Welcome to the TOEIC® L&R Test

—New Edition—

Yoshio Kitahara

Asahi Press

音声再生アプリ「リスニング・トレーナー」を使った音声ダウンロード

朝日出版社開発のアプリ、「リスニング・トレーナー（リストレ）」を使えば、教科書の音声をスマホ、タブレットに簡単にダウンロードできます。どうぞご活用ください。

◉ アプリ【リスニング・トレーナー】の使い方

《アプリのダウンロード》

App Store または Google Play から「リスニング・トレーナー」のアプリ（無料）をダウンロード

App Storeはこちら▶ 　　Google Playはこちら▶

《アプリの使い方》

① アプリを開き「コンテンツを追加」をタップ
② 画面上部に【15649】を入力しDoneをタップ

音声ストリーミング配信 ≫≫

この教科書の音声は、右記ウェブサイトにて無料で配信しています。

　https://text.asahipress.com/free/english/

はしがき

　ようこそ、TOEIC®へ。このテキストは、大学に入学して初めてTOEIC®に挑戦しようとする人や少しだけ勉強したことがある人など、主に入門レベルの人たちを対象としたものです。

　TOEIC® (Test of English for International Communication) とは、英文和訳や和文英訳などの能力ではなく、身近なところからビジネスシーンにいたるまでの幅広い場面における、英語によるコミュニケーション能力を測定するために開発された世界共通のテストです。日本では「(財)国際ビジネスコミュニケーション協会」により運営され、1979年から実施されています。社会的評価も高く、公開テストでの個人受験はもとより、学校、官公庁、企業などさまざまな団体で幅広く活用されています。活用例としては、学校では授業の効果測定、クラス分け、単位認定の基準、入学試験など、また、企業では英語研修の効果測定、海外出張や駐在の基準、昇進の要件などをあげることができます。

　以前は、TOEIC®と言えば、リスニング・セクションとリーディング・セクションからなるものだけでした。しかし、時代の趨勢を背景に、新たにTOEIC® Speaking & Writing Tests(スピーキング約20分間とライティング約60分間のテスト、2007年1月から)なども実施されるようになり、以前からあるものはTOEIC® Listening & Reading Testという名称になっています。本書は、このTOEIC® Listening & Reading Testを対象としたものです。

　TOEIC® Listening & Reading Testについて(財)国際ビジネスコミュニケーション協会が公式ホームページ (URL：https://www.iibc-global.org/toeic.html) で公表している資料によれば、1990年代中頃から急激に受験者数が増加し、2011年度にはまた急激に増加して(2010年度の約178万人に対して約227万人)、2018年度には約245万人(公開テスト約121万人、団体受験約124万人)もの人が受験しています。これも、TOEIC®に対する社会的評価の向上を反映してのことだと思います。

　TOEIC® Listening & Reading Testでの評価は、合否ではなく、リスニング・セクション、リーディング・セクションともそれぞれ5〜495点、トータル10点〜990点のスコアによりおこなわれます。このスコア算出には評価基準を一定に保つための工夫がなされていて、能力に変化がないかぎりスコアも一定に保たれるようになっています。TOEIC® Listening & Reading Test全体の問題構成や2つのセクションを構成する各パートの実際の問題など詳しいことについては、次の「各パートの紹介と本書の編集方針」で述べています。

　最後になりますが、本書を刊行するにあたっては、朝日出版社第一編集部の朝日英一郎氏、小川洋一郎氏、加藤愛理氏をはじめ編集部の皆様にたいへんお世話になりました。朝日氏と小川氏からは、貴重なご助言をいただきました。また、加藤氏からは、企画の段階から完成に至るまでのさまざまな場面において、細やかなご支援をいただきました。これらの方々のおかげで、本書もよりよいものになったと思います。ここに記して、深く感謝いたします。

2019年6月　東北大学　北原 良夫

　それでは、TOEIC® Listening & Reading Testについて詳しく見てみましょう。まず、全体の問題構成ですが、次の表のようになっています。

【TOEIC® Listening & Reading Test全体の問題構成】

	パート	問題の種類	問題数	時 間	点 数
リスニング	1	Photographs（写真描写問題）	6	45 分	495 点
	2	Question-Response（応答問題）	25		
	3	Conversations（会話問題）	39		
	4	Talks（説明文問題）	30		
リーディング	5	Incomplete Sentences（単文穴埋め問題）	30	75 分	495 点
	6	Text Completion（長文穴埋め問題）	16		
	7	Reading Comprehension（読解問題） ・Single passages（1 つの文書） ・Multiple passages（複数の文書）	29 25		
合 計			200	120 分	990 点

　次に、各パートについて、さらに少し詳しく見てみましょう。【問題例】を見ながら各パートの問題の説明をよく読んで、問題形式をしっかり確認してください。

【リスニング・セクション】

◆パート1：写真描写問題

　写真を見て4つの短い説明文を聴き、写真の内容にもっとも合っている説明文を選ぶ問題です。説明文は問題冊子に印刷されていません。

【パート1の問題例】

1.

〈 放送される指示と説明文の4つの選択肢 〉

Look at the picture marked number 1 in your test book.

(A) People are gathering. （人々が集まっている）

(B) People are exercising. （人々が運動をしている）

(C) People are driving. （人々が運転をしている）

(D) People are shopping. （人々が買物をしている）

◆パート2：応答問題

　発話に対して適切な応答になるように、3つの英文からもっともふさわしいものを選ぶ問題です。発話も3つの英文も問題冊子に印刷されていません。

【パート2の問題例】

〈 放送される発話と応答の3つの選択肢 〉

Where are we supposed to hold the conference?

（どこで会議を開催することになっていますか？）

(A) About 3,000. （約3,000です）

(B) In the main conference room. （大会議室です）

(C) It'll be finished really soon. （それはすぐに終わります）

◆パート3：会話問題

　2人または3人の人物による対話を聴き、内容についての設問に答える問題です。1つの対話について設問が3つずつあります。問題冊子に印刷されている図などから読みとった情報も合わせて考えなければならない設問も数問あります。設問と選択肢(4つ) は問題冊子に印刷されています(設問は放送もされます)。

【パート3の問題例】

〈 放送される指示と対話 〉

● Questions 32-34 refer to the following conversation.

W: Well, how did you like the movie?

　　（さて、この映画どうだった？）

M: I thought the acting was good, but the story line was not very realistic.

（演出はよかったと思うけど、ストーリーには現実味があまりなかったね）

W: Hmm, I liked the story, even though it was a bit scary for me. I really liked the way it turned out in the end. And I agree with you about the acting. Pablo Cruz was great as the bad guy.

（ふ〜ん、私にはちょっと怖い内容だったけど、ストーリーはよかったわ。最後の種明かしのところがすごくよかった。それに、演出の点はあなたと同じ意見だわ。パブロ・クルーズは、悪人を演じさせると上手よね）

M: Yes, he is always good. He's been doing romantic comedies recently, so this was different for him.

（ああ、彼はいつも演技がうまいよね。最近はずっとラブ・コメディーばかり出ていたから、この作品は彼にとっても違ってたんじゃないかな）

W: We should rent some of his older movies, like the science fiction one from seven years ago.

（彼が出ている以前の映画を何本か借りて見なくちゃ。7年前のSF映画とか）

32. What did the man think of the movie?　（男性は映画をどう思いましたか？）

(A) It was not funny.　（おもしろくなかった）

(B) It was not scary.　（怖くなかった）

(C) It was not realistic.　（現実味がなかった）

(D) It was not well-acted.　（演出がそれほどうまくなかった）

(A)　(B)　(C)　(D)

33. What does the woman say about an actor?　（女性は俳優についてどう言っていますか？）

(A) He is going to quit acting.　（俳優をやめるつもりだ）

(B) He is usually in romantic comedies.　（彼はいつもラブ・コメディーに出ている）

(C) He might visit her town soon.　（女性が住む町に近々来るかもしれない）

(D) He played a bad guy.　（彼は悪役を演じた）

(A)　(B)　(C)　(D)

34. What does the woman suggest doing?　（女性は何しようと言っていますか？）

(A) Looking for more information about the actor.　（男優についてさらに情報を探す）

(B) Reading a science fiction book.　（SF小説を読む）

(C) Renting some old movies.　（以前の映画を何本か借りる）

(D) Seeing another movie at the theater.　（映画館で別の映画を見る）

(A)　(B)　(C)　(D)

　挨拶や電話などのさまざまな種類の文章を聴き、内容についての設問に答える問題です。1つの文章に対して設問が3つずつあります。問題冊子に印刷されている図などから読みとった情報も合わせて考えなければならない設問も数問あります。設問と選択肢（4つ）は問題冊子に印刷されています（設問は放送もされます）。

【パート4の問題例】

〈 放送される指示と文章 〉

● **Questions 71 through 73 refer to the following announcement.**

We have some great specials in our store today to celebrate our 10th anniversary in this location. First, in our meat section, we have chicken breasts for $3.50 per package. That's 30-percent off. In the deli section, you can get sandwiches or boxed lunches for just $5 each. These are handy to take on a picnic. Over in the dairy section, all of our European cheese is 50-percent off. Don't miss the great selection. And, finally, in produce, pick up a bag of apples for just $7. These are sweet yellow apples from New Zealand. Thank you for shopping at Max's.

（当地開店10周年を記念して、本日当店では一部お買い得品を販売いたします。まず、肉コーナーでは、鶏胸肉を1パッケージ3ドル50セントでご用意しております。30％のお値引きです。総菜コーナーでは、サンドイッチかお弁当をたった5ドルでお買い求めいただけます。ピクニックにお持ちいただくにはお手頃です。むこうの乳製品コーナーでは、ヨーロッパ製チーズがすべて半額です。極上品ですので、お買い忘れのないようお願いいたします。そして最後ですが、リンゴ1袋がたったの7ドルです。ニュー・ジーランド産の甘い黄色リンゴです。マックスをご利用いただきありがとうございます）

71. Why is the store having a sale?　　（なぜこの店ではセールをおこなうのか？）

　　(A)　It is their anniversary.　　（記念祭のため）

　　(B)　It is getting rid of old stock.　　（在庫整理のため）

　　(C)　It is going to close soon.　　（近々閉店するため）

　　(D)　It is their grand opening.　　（開店大売り出しのため）　　

72. What discount can shoppers get on chicken?　　（鶏肉の値引きはどれくらいか？）

　　(A)　10 percent　　（10％）

　　(B)　15 percent　　（15％）

　　(C)　30 percent　　（30％）

　　(D)　50 percent　　（50％）

73. Where did the speaker say the apples came from? （リンゴの産地はどこか？）

    (A) Germany　（ドイツ）

    (B) Japan　（日本）

    (C) New Zealand　（ニュー・ジーランド）

    (D) The U.S.　（アメリカ合衆国）

【リーディング・セクション】

◆パート5：短文穴埋め問題

　語いや熟語、語法、文法事項についての空所補充問題です。選択肢は4つです。

【パート5の問題例】

The review of programs at an educational institution _____ occurs every five years.

　（教育機関における教育プログラムの審査は、一般的に5年に1度おこなわれる）

    (A) general

    (B) generalization

    (C) generalize

    (D) generally

◆パート6：長文穴埋め問題

　内容的にはパート5と同様の語いや熟語、語法、文法事項についての空所補充問題3問と文補充問題1問で構成され、それが文章の中で問われます（パート5は単文）。文章中の空所ですので、適切な語句や文を補充するためには、前後の文脈を考慮しなければならない場合もあります。選択肢は、それぞれの空所に対して4つです。

【パート6の問題例】

● **Questions 131-134 refer to the following notice.**

We have changed our menu to include _____ food from the local area. _____. These
           131.   **132.**
range from shellfish appetizers to dinner fillets of the finest locally-caught fish. Our
seafood dishes are made with unusual spices _____ served in unique combinations.
                    133.
We don't mind "breaking the rules" of traditional cooking a bit if we think we can do
better. Our head chef says his experience cooking in Malta helped _____ come up with
                       134.
the new dishes.

（当店では、地元の食材をもっと利用するようメニューを変更いたしました。新たにご提供する魚貝料理では、地元でとれた多種多様な新鮮な魚を使っております。貝や甲殻類を使った前菜から、地元でとれた最上級の魚のディナー用切り身料理に至るまで、さまざまな料理をご用意しております。当店の魚貝料理は、珍しい香辛料を使っておりますし、当店独自の組み合わせでご提供しております。当店では、より美味しい料理をご提供できるなら、伝統的な調理法での決まりを破ることなど少しも気にしておりません。当店の料理長の話では、マルタ島でコックをしていた経験から今回の新しい料理を思いついたのだそうです。）

---

131. (A) another

    (B) full

    (C) many

    (D) more   Ⓐ Ⓑ Ⓒ **Ⓓ**

132. (A) If you are interested in holding a large gathering here, please talk to your server.

    (B) The great variety of fresh fish in this region is reflected in our new seafood dishes.

    (C) The menu will be changed seasonally, starting next month with our Spring Desserts.

    (D) Our restaurant is now staying open one hour later on weekends, until 11:00 p.m.

        Ⓐ **Ⓑ** Ⓒ Ⓓ

133. (A) and

    (B) so

    (C) that

    (D) when   **Ⓐ** Ⓑ Ⓒ Ⓓ

134. (A) he

    (B) him

    (C) himself

    (D) his   Ⓐ **Ⓑ** Ⓒ Ⓓ

電子メール、短いメッセージのやり取り、オンライン・チャット、ウェブ・ページ、手紙、FAX文書、掲示、広告、新聞や雑誌の記事、レストランのメニューなど、さまざまな種類の英語の文書を読み、内容についての設問に答える問題です。文書が1つの場合と、2つ以上の場合があります。また、文書には、表などが含まれる場合もあります。設問は、文書の数や長さなどに応じて、2〜5問です。選択肢は、1つの設問に対して4つずつあります。設問の中には、文書内に新たな1文を挿入する位置を解答させるものも若干含まれています。

【パート7の問題例】

● **Questions 147-149 refer to the following Web site.**

http://www.nationalrailway.com/spring_of_youth_notice.html/

National Railway has decided to expand on our most popular promotional ticket, the "Spring of Youth" Travel Ticket. We had only offered this ticket in August, but we had such a good response from it that we decided to make it available in December and May. The price will remain at $115 (plus tax), and the conditions of use will also remain the same (see here).

The "Spring of Youth" ticket gives you 5 days of unlimited travel for only $115 (plus tax) in two more months out of the year! And remember, though it is called "Spring of Youth," anyone, regardless of age, can enjoy this inexpensive way to ride the train all over the country.

（国鉄では、当社でもっとも人気の特典乗車券「若者の春」の販売を拡大することにいたしました。従来8月のみの販売でしたが、たいへんご好評でしたので、12月と5月にもご利用いただけるようにいたしました。販売価格は115ドル（税抜）のままで、ご利用条件にも変更はございません（こちらをご覧ください）

「若者の春」乗車券をご利用いただけば、1年のうちさらに2ヶ月間も、5日間無制限で鉄道をご利用いただけます。「若者の春」という名称ではありますが、年齢に関係なくどなたでも、全国どこでも安価に鉄道旅行をお楽しみいただけることをお忘れなく）

147. Why did the company decide to make a change?　（なぜ変更することにしたのか？）

    (A)　Due to a change in company goals　（会社の目標が変わったため）

    (B)　Due to an evaluation of profits　（利益の評価に基づいて）

    (C)　Due to complaints from customers　（利用者からのクレームに対応して）

    (D)　Due to positive feedback from customers　（利用者に好評だったため）

        Ⓐ　Ⓑ　Ⓒ　**Ⓓ**

148. What will change about the promotional ticket?　（特典乗車券のどこが変わったのか？）

    (A)　The age at which one can use it　（利用できる年齢）

    (B)　The length of the train trip　（利用できる距離）

    (C)　The price it sells for　（販売価格）

    (D)　The time it can be used　（利用できる時期）

        Ⓐ　Ⓑ　Ⓒ　**Ⓓ**

149. For how long is the "Spring of Youth" ticket good?　（「若者の春」乗車券の有効期間は？）

    (A)　Five days　（5日間）

    (B)　A week　（1週間）

    (C)　A month　（1ヶ月間）

    (D)　A year　（1年間）

        Ⓐ　Ⓑ　Ⓒ　Ⓓ

　さて、「はしがき」でも述べたように、TOEIC® Listening & Reading Test では合否ではなくスコアにより評価がおこなわれます。では、いったいどれくらいのスコアをめざせばよいのでしょう。目標は高い方がよいのかもしれませんが、高すぎて現実味がない目標も考えものです。入門レベルの学習者であれば、まずは「500 点」を目標にしてみてください。国際ビジネスコミュニケーション協会が公表している資料に「Proficiency Scale」というものがあります。これは、TOEIC® Listening & Reading Test のスコアとコミュニケーション能力のレベルとの相関を示した表です（詳しくは、国際ビジネスコミュニケーション協会のホームページを参照してください。相関表の URL は「https://www.iibc-global.org/library/default/toeic/official_data/lr/pdf/proficiency.pdf」です）。レベルは A 〜 E の 5 つあり（A がもっとも高い）、中間の C レベル（日常生活のニーズを充足し、限定された範囲内では業務上のコミュニケーションができるレベル）がまずめざすべき目標です。TOEIC® Listening & Reading Test のスコアでは「470 点〜 730 点」になります。そこで、まずは切りよく「500 点」という目標を掲げたわけです。なお、この相関表のほかに、「Score

Descriptor Table（レベル別評価の一覧表）」という資料もあり、これも学習に役立つと思います（URL:
https://www.iibc-global.org/toeic/test/lr/guide04/guide04_02/score_descriptor.html）。リスニング・
セクションとリーディング・セクションそれぞれのスコア別に、そのレベルでの長所と短所を一覧
にしたものです。特に、弱点克服にはたいへん有効だと思います。

　ところで、「500点」と言えば満点（990点）の半分くらいですが、これくらいのスコアをとるた
めには（5割ではなく）6割程度正解しなければなりません。TOEIC® Listening & Reading Test
ではそういう仕組みになっています。6割正解というとけっこうたいへんそうに思えますが、入門
レベルの学習者にとってもけっして無理な目標ではありません。ただし、そのためには「戦略」が
重要です。リスニング・セクションでは、比較的易しいパート1とパート2でできるだけ取りこぼ
しを少なくし、比較的難しいパート3と4でできるだけ得点のかさ上げをする必要があります。パー
ト1とパート2の計31問で25問（約8割）正解したとすれば、パート3と4の計69問で半分程度（35
問程度）正解すれば、目標の6割になります。そして、パート1と2でそれくらい正解できる力が
あれば、パート3と4で半分程度正解するのもけっして難しいことではないと思います（パート3
と4では、設問と選択肢があらかじめわかっていますから、対話や文章のすみずみまで聴きとるこ
とは難しくても、設問に関係する部分だけは聞きのがさないようにすればよいのですから）。そこで、
このテキストでは、まずパート1と2についてしっかり練習して力をつけてもらうために、各ユニッ
トともこれらのパートの比重を高めにしています。さらに、パート3と4については、まず設問に
関係する部分をしっかり聴きとる練習をしてもらうために、大部分のユニットで、対話や文章を短
めにし、また、1つの対話や文章に対して設問も1つだけにしてあります（後ろの方のユニット10
〜12には、対話や文章が長めだったり、設問も2つだったりと、少し難度の高い問題も、本番に
近い練習をしてもらうために収録してあります）。

　次に、リーディング・セクションですが、パート5と6については、正確さは言うまでもありま
せんが、できるだけスピーディーに解き（特に問題数の多いパート5）、パート7に使える時間をで
きるだけ多くするのが理想です。パート7では解答に時間を必要とする設問も多くありますが、言
い方を換えれば、時間さえかければ正解できる場合も少なくありません。パート5と6で時間を使
いすぎ（特にパート5）、パート7が中途半端で終わってしまう、というのが典型的に悪いパターン
のひとつです。その上、パート5と6の正解率が低かったら、目もあてられないことになりますね。

　パート5とパート6の計46問で35問（約7割5分）正解したとすれば、パート7の54問で半
分弱程度（25問程度）正解すれば目標の6割になります。繰り返しになりますが、パート7では
時間さえかければ正解できる場合も少なくありませんので、このパートで半分弱程度正解するのは
けっして難しいことではないと思います。ポイントは、パート7にどれくらい多くの時間を配分で
きるか、です。そのためには、パート5と6をできるだけ正確かつ迅速に解答していけるよう、語
いや熟語、語法、文法事項に関する知識をできるだけたくさん身につける必要があります。パー
ト5や6では、文全体の意味や文脈をあまり考えなくても、単純な知識だけで、極端な場合ほんの

数秒で解ける問題もけっして少なくありません。そこで，このテキストでは，問題数の多いパート5についてまずしっかり練習して力をつけてもらうために、各ユニットともこのパートの比重を高めにしています。一方、パート7については、さまざまな内容やスタイルの文章に触れてもらうとともに、問題を解く「感触」をつかんでもらうことを主な目的としています。そのため、文章も短めにし、また、設問数も少なめにした問題を中心にしています（後ろの方のユニット9〜12には、文章が複数で長めだったり、設問数も多めだったりと、少し難度の高い問題も、本番に近い練習をしてもらうために収録してあります）。

　各ユニットのリスニング・セクションとリーディング・セクションの前には、それぞれ「語いの確認」があります（リスニング・セクションの前の「語いの確認」は、リスニングのウォームアップも兼ねて聴きとり式にしてあります）。ここで扱われている単語は、TOEIC® Listening & Reading Test でよく出てくるものばかりです。しっかり覚えてください。

　このテキストの構成について、最後にもうひとつだけ。各ユニットの最後には、「文法チェック」と「学習のヒント」があります。「文法チェック」は、そのユニットのパート5で扱われている文法事項についてまとめたものです（同じ文法事項が複数のユニットで扱われている場合もあります）。スペースの関係で、パート5の問題に沿った簡単なまとめにならざるをえませんが、パート5で間違いが多かったときには、その文法事項について手持ちの参考書などを利用し幅広く確認しておくことをお勧めします。授業の担当教員によってこのテキストの使い方はいろいろだと思いますが、パート5については、まずこの「文法チェック」に目を通して知識の確認や整理をしてから、実際に問題を解いてみるのもひとつの方法です。一方、「学習のヒント」は、各パートの問題への取り組み方をはじめ、TOEIC® Listening & Reading Test に対する取り組み方をまとめたものです。やはりスペースの関係から、各ユニットに分散させて収録してありますが、できれば、このテキストを使って学習を始める前に一通り目を通しておいてください。このテキストでの学習が、より効果的なものになると思います。

　改めて、TOEIC® へようこそ！　このテキストを使って学習される学生の皆さんが、TOEIC® の攻略に必要となるベースを身につけられるよう願っています。

Contents

Welcome to the TOEIC® L&R Test

—New Edition—

Unit 1

🎧 **LISTENING** 〽6

●●○ **Warm-up & Vocabulary Build-up** ○●●

英文を聴きとって、空所にあてはまる単語を下の選択肢から選んで入れなさい。

1. Some people are _____ across from the river.
2. A waiter is _____ food to the table at the restaurant.
3. Is fax paper on our shopping list for office _____?
4. How did you become _____ with computers?
5. Would you tell me what this technical _____ means?
6. She _____ worried about our deadline, doesn't she?
7. You can also use a taxi _____ of the subway.
8. This children's medicine has a cherry _____.

    a. familiar   **b.** flavor   **c.** instead   **d.** serving

    e. sounds   **f.** supplies   **g.** term   **h.** waving

---

Part 1   **Photographs**

You will hear four short statements. Look at the picture, and select the statement that best describes what you see in the picture.

1.

    (A) (B) (C) (D)

2.

(A)　(B)　(C)　(D)

3.

(A)　(B)　(C)　(D)

Part 2   Question-Response

You will hear a question or statement and three responses. Listen carefully, and select the best response to the question or statement.

4. (A) (B) (C)

5. (A) (B) (C)

6. (A) (B) (C)

7. (A) (B) (C)

8. (A) (B) (C)

Part 3   Conversations

You will hear a short conversation between two people. Listen carefully, and select the best response to each question.

9. What are they discussing?
    (A) Where to meet   (B) Doing the laundry
    (C) The weather   (D) Clothing

10. What will the speakers do?
    (A) Go to the store   (B) Visit the museum
    (C) Go to the space lab   (D) See an SF movie

11. Why doesn't the woman want to go?
    (A) She went out yesterday.   (B) She has something to do.
    (C) She feels tired.   (D) She doesn't like going out.

Part 4   Talks

You will hear a short talk given by a single speaker. Listen carefully, and select the best response to each question.

12. Where would this announcement be heard?
    (A) In a bank   (B) In a library
    (C) At an airport   (D) In a hospital

13. Where is this announcement being made?
    (A) In Winston   (B) At a station
    (C) In a park   (D) On a train

14. Who is the message aimed at?
    (A) Busy women   (B) Stereo fans
    (C) Desk workers   (D) Clothing shoppers

📖 READING

●●● Vocabulary Build-up ●●●

空所にあてはまる単語を、下の選択肢から選んで入れなさい。

1. _____ stores sell single items to shoppers.
2. This handbook _____ all company rules.
3. I _____ coffee on the keyboard by mistake.
4. Dan could not _____ the loud music next-door.
5. This class will _____ many aspects of the local history.
6. That apartment has been _____ long since Kenny moved out.
7. I know that you're _____ about losing your job.
8. I need a piece of cloth to _____ the table.

a. explains	**b.** provide	**c.** retail	**d.** spilled
e. stand	**f.** upset	**g.** vacant	**h.** wipe

Part 5 　Incomplete Sentences

A word or phrase is missing in each of the sentences. Select the best answer to complete each sentence.

15. He _____ his father.
    (A) resembles
    (B) resembles to
    (C) resembles with
    (D) resembles on

16. We have had exceptionally good weather since we _____ in this country.
    (A) reached
    (B) left
    (C) arrived
    (D) went

17. I usually _____ soccer with my friends on weekends.
    (A) play
    (B) plays
    (C) playing
    (D) was playing

18. No one _____ how the pyramids in Egypt were built.
    (A) known
    (B) knowing
    (C) know
    (D) knows

19. Buy the best quality even if it _____ something that is not trendy.
    (A) were
    (B) was
    (C) be
    (D) is

20. Mother's watch could not be _____.

    (A) expired   (B) delayed

    (C) repaired   (D) confirmed

21. Which part of the test _____ the most difficult for you?

    (A) had   (B) was

    (C) did   (D) made

22. When you are in London, where will you _____?

    (A) hold   (B) stay

    (C) break   (D) leave

23. The purse did not _____ to anyone in the room.

    (A) want   (B) belong

    (C) hope   (D) respond

24. Get _____ the train at the Green Station.

    (A) off   (B) by

    (C) out   (D) from

Part 6 — Text Completion

Read the text that follows. A word, phrase, or sentence is missing in parts of the text. Select the best answer to complete the text.

● Questions 25-28 refer to the following advertisement.

WE'VE GOT HUNDREDS OF USED CARS PRICED TO SELL!

★ ★ ★

Smith Motors needs to sell our entire stock of _____ cars by 9:00 P.M. this

25.

Sunday. We have economy cars, sedans, and trucks all at the _____ possible

26.

prices. _____. If you've been thinking about buying a used car, this is the time

27.

you've been waiting _____. Don't miss out!

28.

25. (A) use

(B) used

(C) useful

(D) usefulness

26. (A) low

(B) lower

(C) lowest

(D) lowly

27. (A) Our taxi service is coming to your town.

(B) Some cars are priced as low as $500.

(C) This is the best car for a large family.

(D) When you need a fast car, think of us.

28. (A) about

(B) for

(C) in

(D) to

Read the following selection of texts. Select the best answer for each question.

●Questions 29-30 refer to the following advertisement.

TOUR GUIDE (PART-TIME)

Do you like traveling? Do you like meeting people?
The WORLD TRAVEL is looking for a healthy and hard working person.
- under 40 years of age
- 2 years experience as tour guide
- work 3 days a week (Mon, Wed, Fri 6 A.M.— 4 P.M.)
- $35.00 per hour
If you are interested, phone the manager at 02-222-6666.

29. Who issued this advertisement?

    (A) Bus company   (B) Drivers

    (C) Tour guides   (D) Travel agency

30. Who is not recommended for this job?

    (A) A person who is healthy   (B) A person who likes traveling

    (C) A person who is 45 years old   (D) A person who works hard

●Questions 31-32 refer to the following notice.

➡ BEFORE YOU ENTER ➡

Visitors are reminded that the use of cameras is not allowed. The bright light from the flash causes the colors of the paintings to fade.

Postcards of all the paintings on display are available and can be bought at the museum kiosk. The money from the sale of these postcards will be used to restore and repair old works of art.

Thank you and enjoy the exhibit.

31. Where would a person see such a notice?

    (A) Near the exit to the museum   (B) At the entrance to the exhibit

    (C) On the back of the entrance ticket   (D) In the lobby of the museum

32. What have visitors to the museum been asked to do?

    (A) Be quiet in the museum   (B) Avoid touching the paintings

    (C) Donate money to the museum   (D) Do not take pictures of the exhibits

文法チェック ✔

●動詞と時制（1）

A. 動詞には自動詞と他動詞があります。他動詞は、目的語（日本語でふつう「〜を」にあたるもの）を従えます。他動詞なのに、日本語に惑わされて、余計な前置詞などを用いないように注意しましょう。たとえば、日本語では「〜について議論する」と言ったりしますが、"discuss 〜" であって "discuss *about* 〜" とは言いません。

例：「〜に近づく」= approach 〜（× approach to 〜）、「〜に似ている」= resemble 〜（× resemble to 〜）、「〜に出席する」= attend 〜（× attend to 〜）、「〜と結婚する」= marry 〜（× marry with 〜）、「〜から立ち去る」= leave 〜（× leave from 〜）など

B. 英語の文には、必ず述語動詞（現在や過去などの「時制」をもった動詞）があります。動詞を補充する問題では、述語動詞なのかをまず確認してみてください。そうであれば、ふさわしい時制を表す動詞形を選ぶだけです。ありえない選択肢は最初から消去できます。時制の形式と意味をしっかり確認しておきましょう。have の後なので過去分詞を補い「現在完了」を完成させる、といった単純な問題もあります。

C. 英語では、主語に応じて述語動詞の形に注意しなければならないことがあります。「三人称単数」主語の場合の -s などです。解答を選ぶときには、主語の人称と数をしっかり確認しましょう。

D. 「現在時制」は、「現在の習慣的行為」（動作動詞の場合）や「現在の状態」（状態動詞の場合）を表します。前者の場合、always、often、usually、sometimes、seldom などの語で、その行為の「頻度」を表すことがよくあります。

学習のヒント

　パート1の写真は、人やものを中心とした「ポートレート風のもの」（1人の人や1つのもの、複数の人やものが比較的大きく写っているもの、など）と、光景や風景を写した「風景写真風のもの」（部屋の様子や建物の外観などが比較的大きく写っているもの、人工物や自然を比較的広い範囲で写したもの、など）です。このテキストでは、前者を主に奇数ユニットで、後者を偶数ユニットで扱っています。

　写っている人やものが多かったり、広い範囲を写したりした「複雑な」内容の写真では、情報量が格段に多くなります。「単純な」内容の写真では、音声と同時に写真を確認していっても間に合います。でも、写真の内容が複雑になるほど、音声と写真との照合に手間がかかり、流れてくる音声についていけなくなったりします。そのため、あらかじめ写真を見ておくことができるどうかで正解率が変わることがあります。音声が流される前にできるだけ写真を見ておく練習を、意識的にしてみてください。

Unit 2

LISTENING

●●● Warm-up & Vocabulary Build-up ●●●

英文を聴きとって、空所にあてはまる単語を下の選択肢から選んで入れなさい。

1. The bridge extends _____ the river.
2. The guards are standing _____ the gate.
3. Does the car have enough _____ for our trip today?
4. We need to _____ a guidebook for new workers.
5. Could I _____ you a cup of coffee?
6. Please leave the bottom part of the _____ empty.
7. From this hilltop, we have an _____ view of the city.
8. This tour will include _____ to visit local markets.

a. across	**b.** beside	**c.** excellent	**d.** form
e. gas	**f.** offer	**g.** opportunities	**h.** prepare

Part 1　　**Photographs**

You will hear four short statements. Look at the picture, and select the statement that best describes what you see in the picture.

1.

(A)　(B)　(C)　(D)

2.

(A)　(B)　(C)　(D)

3.

(A)　(B)　(C)　(D)

You will hear a question or statement and three responses. Listen carefully, and select the best response to the question or statement.

4. (A) (B) (C)

5. (A) (B) (C)

6. (A) (B) (C)

7. (A) (B) (C)

8. (A) (B) (C)

Part 3   **Conversations**

You will hear a short conversation between two people. Listen carefully, and select the best response to each question.

9. Where are they?
    (A) At a restaurant   (B) In a clothing store
    (C) At a dry cleaner's   (D) Inside a grocery store

10. How did the man come to work today?
    (A) By bus   (B) By car
    (C) By subway   (D) On foot

11. What will the man do?
    (A) Leave a message   (B) Visit Julia
    (C) Go out to look for Julia   (D) Call again later

Part 4   **Talks**

You will hear a short talk given by a single speaker. Listen carefully, and select the best response to each question.

12. Where can this announcement be heard?
    (A) At a tow-truck company   (B) At a car dealership
    (C) At a locksmith's shop   (D) At a store's parking lot

13. What is being announced?
    (A) Longer operating hours   (B) A holiday sale
    (C) A one-month closure   (D) A shorter work schedule

14. Where is this announcement being made?
    (A) Aboard Flight 689   (B) At the customs area
    (C) At the baggage claim area   (D) At a boarding gate

READING

●●● Vocabulary Build-up ●●●

空所にあてはまる単語を、下の選択肢から選んで入れなさい。

1. The _____ for this idea goes to Ellen.
2. Rain has _____ painting the house.
3. The meal comes with the _____ of soup or salad.
4. Don _____ that his interview went well.
5. The speech covered both _____ and foreign issues.
6. There has been little _____ of this team in the news.
7. I have time to write only a short _____.
8. Which _____ lane has the shortest line of shoppers?

a. checkout   b. coverage   c. credit   d. domestic

e. interrupted   f. note   g. option   h. remarked

Part 5   Incomplete Sentences

A word or phrase is missing in each of the sentences. Select the best answer to complete each sentence.

15. As soon as the hotel _____, every room will be completely filled.

(A) will open   (B) opens
(C) opened   (D) had opened

16. The sale starts tomorrow and _____ through the weekend.

(A) run   (B) will run
(C) to run   (D) being run

17. We _____ on the phone when we heard the noise outside.

(A) talk   (B) talks
(C) are talking   (D) were talking

18. Linda has never _____ to Europe.

(A) being   (B) be
(C) was   (D) been

19. He _____ studying at the library since lunch today.

(A) has been   (B) is
(C) had been   (D) will be

20. The city is _____ by hills.

    (A) next   (B) near

    (C) known   (D) surrounded

21. I believe the phone has not _____ since I got here this morning.

    (A) called   (B) replied

    (C) dialed   (D) rung

22. Cars and trucks mainly _____ this bridge to cross over the river.

    (A) call   (B) stop

    (C) use   (D) go

23. Four local high schools _____ the city sports festival in turn.

    (A) to host   (B) are hosts

    (C) hosts of   (D) host

24. Jim was late for school today because his bicycle _____ down.

    (A) stopped   (B) broke

    (C) failed   (D) crashed

Part 6 　　Text Completion

Read the text that follows. A word, phrase, or sentence is missing in parts of the text. Select the best answer to complete the text.

●Questions 25-28 refer to the following information.

Come enjoy a special evening at Harmony Fashion.

On Tuesday, December 6 from 7:00 P.M. to 9:00 P.M., we'll be featuring live harp music, plus a short fashion show of the L. Marcu Collection. There will also be appetizers _____ fun prizes. Get a preview of _____ winter's fashions
　　　　　　　　　25. 　　　　　　　　　　　　　　　　　　　**26.**
and spend a nice evening with us. _____. There will _____ a $10 cover
　　　　　　　　　　　　　　　　27. 　　　　　　　　　　**28.**
charge.

25. (A) and
　　　(B) but
　　　(C) for
　　　(D) so

26. (A) past
　　　(B) such
　　　(C) that
　　　(D) this

27. (A) Call early to reserve your space.
　　　(B) Choose from small or medium sizes.
　　　(C) Everything is on sale this weekend.
　　　(D) We will be closed for renovations.

28. (A) be
　　　(B) have
　　　(C) see
　　　(D) want

Read the following selection of texts. Select the best answer for each question.

●Questions 29-30 refer to the following article.

Doctor died of SARS

A 30-year-old woman doctor, Cheng died of SARS. She was infected by a SARS patient and had been in hospital since 21 April. Cheng worked in the department of medicine and voluntarily joined the SARS team. Cheng was the second public hospital doctor to die of SARS in Hong Kong. SARS has killed 281 people and sickened 1742 people in Hong Kong, including 384 health-care workers.

---

29. How many people died of SARS in Hong Kong?

    (A) 281 people   (B) 1742 people

    (C) 384 people   (D) None

30. Which is true about this article?

    (A) Lots of SARS patients were infected by Cheng.

    (B) Cheng voluntarily worked in the SARS team.

    (C) Cheng was the only doctor who died of SARS.

    (D) SARS is not a serious disease.

●Questions 31-33 refer to the following graph.

The Sun Herald conducted the survey in June 2003. 1000 boys and girls between 10 and 17 years of age answered about their roles in housework.

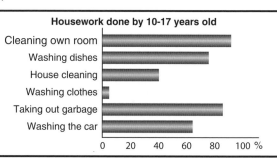

Housework done by 10-17 years old

---

31. What is this survey about?

    (A) Boys and girls' roles in housework (B) Boys and girls' part-time jobs

    (C) Boys and girls' pocket money   (D) Boys and girls' favorite activities

32. Which housework do the boys and girls do most?

    (A) Washing dishes   (B) House cleaning

    (C) Cleaning own room   (D) Washing the car

33. Which is true about this survey?

    (A) 40% of them wash the dishes.   (B) Most of them clean their own rooms.

    (C) Most of them wash clothes.   (D) This survey was conducted by parents.

文法チェック ✓

●動詞と時制 (2)

A. 「時」や「条件」を表す副詞節では、未来のことでも現在時制で表します。

　　例：Let's go out when she *is* ready.

　　　（彼女の準備ができたら出かけましょう）

　　また、次の例のような違いに注意しましょう。

　　例：We'll go on a picnic if it *is* fine tomorrow.　[if 以下は「条件」を表す副詞節]

　　　（明日天気がよかったらピクニックに行きます）

　　例：I'm not sure if it *will be* fine tomorrow.　[if 以下は副詞節ではない]

　　　（明日天気がよくなるかわからない）

B. 現在完了 (have [has] 過去分詞) は、現在までの「動作の完了・結果」、「経験」、「状態の継続」を表します。

C. 「状態の継続」ではなく「動作の継続」を表すには現在完了進行形 (have [has] been 〜 ing) を用います。

D. （現在完了や現在完了進行形に限らず）完了形や完了進行形では、その意味に応じて典型的に用いられる副詞 (句) があります。「動作の完了・結果」では already、just、not ... yet など、「経験」では ever、never など、「状態・動作の継続」では「期間」を表すもの、などです。こういった副詞 (句) を覚えておくと問題が解きやすくなります。間違いやすいのは just now で、これは現在完了とともに用いることはできません。

　　例：I came (×have come) here *just now*.

　　　（私はたった今ここに来たところです）

学習のヒント

　パート1では、人やものについて「どういう様子なのか」（人の場合なら「誰が何をしているのか」）がよく問われますので、集中的に練習できるよう、このテキストでも多く扱っています。「誰が／何が」（主語の部分）と「どういう様子なのか」（動詞の部分）をしっかり聴きとりましょう。

　また、人が複数人の場合、識別情報（つまり、主語の前後にある修飾表現）が重要になる場合もあります（【Unit 7 問2】、【Unit 9 問2】、【Unit 11 問2】など）。「何を身につけているか」、「どこにいるか」といった情報です。この部分も注意して聴きとることができるよう、意識して練習してみてください。

　位置関係（どこに誰がいるのか／何があるのか）が問われることもよくあります（【Unit 2 問1、問2】、【Unit 6 問1、問2】など）。ユニット1の「学習のヒント」で「音声が流される前にできるだけ写真を見ておくこと」を勧めましたが、その際には上下、左右、前後、内外といった位置関係も注意して見ておくようにしましょう。

Unit 3

🎧 LISTENING

●●• Warm-up & Vocabulary Build-up •●●

英文を聴きとって、空所にあてはまる単語を下の選択肢から選んで入れなさい。

1. The classroom looks _____ without desks and chairs.
2. The road runs _____ with the river.
3. Would you _____ me to your boss?
4. Do you _____ this number is correct?
5. We can _____ money by taking fewer trips.
6. Many people lost their jobs when the _____ closed.
7. This _____ goes to the student with the best grades.
8. The plane _____ at the airport five minutes ago.

a. award	**b.** bare	**c.** factory	**d.** introduce
e. landed	**f.** parallel	**g.** save	**h.** suppose

Part 1　Photographs

You will hear four short statements. Look at the picture, and select the statement that best describes what you see in the picture.

1.

(A)　(B)　(C)　(D)

2.

(A) (B) (C) (D)

3.

(A) (B) (C) (D)

You will hear a question or statement and three responses. Listen carefully, and select the best response to the question or statement.

4. (A) (B) (C)

5. (A) (B) (C)

6. (A) (B) (C)

7. (A) (B) (C)

8. (A) (B) (C)

Part 3 Conversations

You will hear a short conversation between two people. Listen carefully, and select the best response to each question.

9. When will the woman go to the play?
    (A) Tonight   (B) Tomorrow night
    (C) Next Saturday   (D) This weekend

10. What did the man think?
    (A) The woman was a customer.   (B) He found a good pair of shoes.
    (C) The woman's uniform was familiar. (D) The customer was an employee.

11. Why does the woman feel sorry?
    (A) She broke a promise.   (B) She bothered Jane Smith.
    (C) She doesn't know Jane.   (D) She dialed the wrong number.

Part 4 Talks

You will hear a short talk given by a single speaker. Listen carefully, and select the best response to each question.

12. What is being announced?
    (A) New subway schedules   (B) New subway prices
    (C) Names of new stations   (D) Subway construction plans

13. What is this announcement about?
    (A) An overbooking   (B) A postponement
    (C) Getting on board   (D) A cancellation

14. What kind of show is this?
    (A) Current affairs   (B) World news
    (C) Athletics   (D) Music

📖 READING

●●● Vocabulary Build-up ●●●

空所にあてはまる単語を、下の選択肢から選んで入れなさい。

1. The teacher will _____ the students' papers.
2. Harry didn't _____ that he had missed his station.
3. She _____ to return his phone calls.
4. He _____ his thoughts clearly.
5. The news was right on every _____.
6. Part-time employees are not _____ for sick pay.
7. Fax _____ times are several seconds per page.
8. This letter is a _____ to your invitation.

a. count	**b.** eligible	**c.** evaluate	**d.** failed
e. notice	**f.** reply	**g.** stated	**h.** transmission

Part 5 — Incomplete Sentences ✏

A word or phrase is missing in each of the sentences. Select the best answer to complete each sentence.

15. This winter has been one of the coldest we _____ in years.
- (A) are having
- (B) had
- (C) will have
- (D) have had

16. I have had the same math teacher _____ two years now.
- (A) by
- (B) after
- (C) since
- (D) for

17. By the time he reached home, he _____ soaked to the skin.
- (A) would be
- (B) was being
- (C) had been
- (D) has been

18. I _____ to get hold of Peter for over a week now.
- (A) will try
- (B) have been trying
- (C) had tried
- (D) will be trying

19. Yesterday, I came across a book which I _____ since I left New York.
- (A) been looking for
- (B) looked for
- (C) was looking for
- (D) had been looking for

20. Please _____ the receptionist your name when you reach our office.

    (A) say   (B) talk

    (C) tell   (D) speak

21. Rice _____ in water during the early part of the farming season.

    (A) adds   (B) makes

    (C) raises   (D) grows

22. An additional office tower was _____ behind the station.

    (A) born   (B) installed

    (C) built   (D) fixed

23. All the rooms in the hotel are _____ because of the big soccer match.

    (A) occupations   (B) occupied

    (C) occupants   (D) occupy

24. Please _____ at the tickets enclosed for further details.

    (A) watch   (B) see

    (C) notice   (D) look

Part 6 ／ Text Completion

Read the text that follows. A word, phrase, or sentence is missing in parts of the text. Select the best answer to complete the text.

●Questions 25-28 refer to the following contract.

The cleaning deposit on the apartment is $900, but if the apartment is _____
　　　　　　　　　　　　　　　　　　　　　　　　　　　　　　　　　　　25.

when you move out, the entire deposit will be refunded. No pets _____
　　　　　　　　　　　　　　　　　　　　　　　　　　　　　　　　　26.

allowed in any of the apartments. The apartment is meant for one person only.

_____. You are asked to respect all your neighbors by keeping
　　　27.

_____ areas clean and keeping noise to a minimum.
　　　28.

---

　25. (A) clean
　　　(B) empty
　　　(C) frozen
　　　(D) happy

　26. (A) are
　　　(B) be
　　　(C) is
　　　(D) were

　27. (A) No additional people are allowed.
　　　(B) Nobody has asked for a refund.
　　　(C) The second month was harder.
　　　(D) You can't hand your paper in late.

　28. (A) common
　　　(B) commonality
　　　(C) commonly
　　　(D) commonness

Read the following selection of texts. Select the best answer for each question.

●Questions 29-30 refer to the following notice.

Overseas Shipping

Latin America costs $6.00 per pound.

For Europe, Africa and Asia, add 50%.

For Australia, add 75%.

Allow 10 days to two weeks for delivery.

*Canada, Mexico, and the Caribbean are charged domestic rates.

Allow 2 or 3 days for delivery.

29. What place is most expensive?

(A) Europe

(B) Africa

(C) The Caribbean

(D) Australia

30. How is Canada different?

(A) It is cheaper than Mexico.

(B) It is not charged as a foreign country.

(C) It has one-day delivery.

(D) It is not served by this company.

●Questions 31-33 refer to the following memo.

Bring this coupon to Linda's Beauty Shop before the end of October. You will get a free treatment. Services covered by the coupon are cutting, coloring, straightening, putting in curls or nail treatment. It is a good idea to make an appointment. Beauty advice is always free at Linda's Beauty Shop.

3422 North Water Street, Akron.

11:00 to 8:00 M-Sat.

(330) 723-9083.

31. What can you get for this coupon?

(A) House repairs

(B) Beauty treatment

(C) A painting

(D) Lawn care

32. What happens at the end of October?

(A) A new carpenter arrives.

(B) The shop will close.

(C) The coupon runs out.

(D) The fall schedule begins.

33. What is the advice?

(A) To wait until November

(B) To use stronger nails

(C) To finish your shopping early

(D) To call before you come in

文法チェック ✔

●動詞と時制 (3)

A. 過去完了 (had 過去分詞) と未来完了 (will have 過去分詞) は、基準時をそれぞれ「過去のある時」と「未来のある時」にしただけで、表す意味や、その意味に応じて典型的に用いられる副詞 (句) は、現在完了の場合と同じです。

B. 過去完了進行形 (had been ～ing) と未来完了進行形 (will have been ～ing) は、基準時をそれぞれ「過去のある時」と「未来のある時」にしただけで、表す意味や、その意味に応じて典型的に用いられる副詞 (句) は、現在完了進行形の場合と同じです。

●品詞

A. 単語を働きなどの点から分類したものを「品詞」と言います。名詞、動詞、形容詞、副詞などがあります。TOEIC® Listening & Reading Test のパート5や6では、どの品詞を補えばよいかがわかると容易に解ける問題もあり、比較的よく出題されます。次の例では、(A)名詞、(B)動詞 (の原形か現在形)、(C)形容詞、(D)副詞のうち、(C)が正解です。空所が be 動詞の補語の位置であり、空所に入る語が副詞 highly により修飾できるものだからです。

例：The attempt was highly (　　). （その試みはたいへんうまくいった）

(A) success　(B) succeed　(C) successful　(D) successfully

B. 単語の中には複数の品詞として用いることができるものもあります。

学習のヒント

　パート2では、問いかけも選択肢も問題冊子には印刷されていません。ですから、「問いかけ」をしっかり聴きとることがたいへん重要になります。「問いかけ」には、疑問詞で始まる疑問文がたいへん多く出題されます。また、「誰の／何のことなのか」(主語の部分) や「いつのことなのか」(動詞の部分) も、正解を選ぶ上では重要です。つまり、最初の数語がたいへん重要になりますので、まずはこの部分をしっかり聴きとることを意識して練習してみてください。特に疑問詞を正確に聴きとることがたいへん重要で、それさえできれば容易に正解できることもよくあります。このテキストでも、以上の点を集中的に練習できるようにしてあります (ユニット5～12)。なお、疑問詞で始まっていても、応答がストレートでないものや、「疑問」以外の意味になっているもの (Why don't you take a rest?「休憩してはどうですか」) などが出題される場合もあります。前者については、このテキストでも練習できるようになっています (【Unit 6 問6】、【Unit 7 問3】など)。

　疑問詞がない疑問文もある程度出題されますが、疑問詞がない点が異なるだけで、「最初の数語にまず集中する」というポイントは同じです。このテキストでは、ユニット1～4で練習するようになっています。「選択疑問」、「付加疑問」、「依頼を表す場合」などいろいろな場合や表現などを確認しながら練習してみてください。

Unit 4

🎧 LISTENING

●●● Warm-up & Vocabulary Build-up ●●●

英文を聴きとって、空所にあてはまる単語を下の選択肢から選んで入れなさい。

1. The _____ leads to the building's entrance.
2. The _____ connects the two lakes.
3. The _____ is receiving money from the customer.
4. Have our sales _____ because of the scandal?
5. Susan left the café in _____ and forgot her umbrella.
6. We _____ payment by credit card or personal check.
7. Do not leave your _____ unattended in the terminal.
8. Please enter the _____ number of the department.

a. accept	**b.** canal	**c.** cashier	**d.** declined
e. extension	**f.** haste	**g.** luggage	**h.** sidewalk

Part 1　　Photographs

You will hear four short statements. Look at the picture, and select the statement that best describes what you see in the picture.

1.

(A)　(B)　(C)　(D)

2.

(A)　(B)　(C)　(D)

3.

(A)　(B)　(C)　(D)

You will hear a question or statement and three responses. Listen carefully, and select the best response to the question or statement.

4. (A) (B) (C)

5. (A) (B) (C)

6. (A) (B) (C)

7. (A) (B) (C)

8. (A) (B) (C)

Part 3 — **Conversations**

You will hear a short conversation between two people. Listen carefully, and select the best response to each question.

9. What will the woman do?
    (A) Go to another store   (B) Pay for some purchases
    (C) Try on some shoes   (D) Look for a shirt

10. Where are the speakers?
    (A) In a restaurant   (B) In a shoe store
    (C) In a bookstore   (D) In a doctor's office

11. What are these two people doing?
    (A) Applying for work at Turinova, Ltd. (B) Riding to work together
    (C) Attending a convention   (D) Meeting for the first time

Part 4 — **Talks**

You will hear a short talk given by a single speaker. Listen carefully, and select the best response to each question.

12. What is being advertised?
    (A) A trip   (B) A restaurant
    (C) A hotel   (D) An event

13. What is this report about?
    (A) Pollution of Edward Lake   (B) Burglaries near the lake
    (C) Police patrols around the lake   (D) Residents who live in the lake area

14. What is happening today?
    (A) A chain store is expanding.   (B) An independent market is closing.
    (C) A man is ending a nationwide trip. (D) A man is turning one hundred.

READING

●●● Vocabulary Build-up ●●●

空所にあてはまる単語を、下の選択肢から選んで入れなさい。

1. Those small details don't _____.
2. The two contest winners _____ the prize money.
3. The _____ weather kept people away from the beach.
4. The book you ordered will arrive in a _____ package.
5. Larry fixes old bicycles and sells them for a large _____.
6. The flight is _____ going to arrive on time.
7. Can you _____ quickly to this e-mail?
8. I know the basic story, but none of the _____.

a. awful	**b.** definitely	**c.** details	**d.** matter
e. profit	**f.** respond	**g.** separate	**h.** split

Part 5 Incomplete Sentences

A word or phrase is missing in each of the sentences. Select the best answer to complete each sentence.

15. It's a good movie. You _____ go and see it.
    (A) will   (B) shall
    (C) could   (D) should

16. The windows aren't dirty. We _____ clean them.
    (A) must   (B) must not
    (C) need to   (D) don't have to

17. The baby was _____ up by a loud noise.
    (A) wake   (B) woke
    (C) woken   (D) waking

18. Somebody broke into my house but nothing _____.
    (A) steal   (B) stole
    (C) was stolen   (D) was stealing

19. If you _____ a little sooner, you would have reached me before I left.
    (A) call   (B) called
    (C) had called   (D) would call

20. Our hotel room was dirty, so we _____ a cleaner one.

    (A) asked   (B) looked

    (C) stayed   (D) requested

21. I cannot _____ his name, but I know I have seen him before.

    (A) know   (B) remind

    (C) teach   (D) recall

22. This is the first time that we have _____ our sales goal.

    (A) exceeded   (B) preceded

    (C) receded   (D) proceeded

23. The cafeteria _____ room for 200 students to sit down.

    (A) is   (B) does

    (C) has   (D) makes

24. During the earthquake, one picture _____ off the wall.

    (A) fell   (B) took

    (C) left   (D) turned

Part 6 **Text Completion**

Read the text that follows. A word, phrase, or sentence is missing in parts of the text. Select the best answer to complete the text.

●Questions 25-28 refer to the following information.

Medical Assistant Course

This 16-week course _____ book learning with practical instruction in clinical
                         25.

medical assisting. Participants will learn from qualified instructors. _____. After
                                26.

completing the course successfully, the _____ will have all the requirements
                            27.

for the job title of Clinical Medical Assistant. Graduates will also be able to take

the _____ Medical Assistant Associations certification exam.
        28.

25. (A) combines
    (B) combining
    (C) had combined
    (D) has been combined

26. (A) Now that you have finished your courses, it's time to look for a job.
    (B) The first four weeks will be focused on how to design simple websites.
    (C) The next step is to download the editing software from the Internet.
    (D) Understanding will be tested by written and practical examinations.

27. (A) athlete
    (B) editor
    (C) graduate
    (D) teacher

28. (A) casual
    (B) optional
    (C) perfect
    (D) strong

Read the following selection of texts. Select the best answer for each question.

● Questions 29-30 refer to the following notice.

MOVING SALE—SATURDAY ONLY

Living room furniture:

large couch (just reupholstered)	—$115
solid oak coffee table	—$65
two matching end tables	—$45 each
antique floor lamp	—$35

Bedroom furniture:

queen-size brass bed frame	—$150
chest of drawers	—$50
dresser with mirror	—$90

We also have a large variety of other items including kitchenware, decorative crafts, gardening tools, and all kinds of clothing. The sale starts at 9:00 A.M., but please don't come early. We need time to set up.

---

29. What is being announced?

(A) A department store sale

(B) A sale at someone's home

(C) An antique auction

(D) A new second-hand store

30. Which of the following would be the most expensive?

(A) The couch and the floor lamp

(B) The chest and the dresser

(C) The three tables

(D) The brass bed

●Questions 31-33 refer to the following letter.

Mr. Nunn,

This reminder is to let you know that the title you checked out on July 17, "Looking for Linda", has been overdue since July 19. Presently, there is a $5.00 late fine for this movie, and the fine will continue to increase at $1.00 per day until you return the DVD to us. In the case the DVD has been damaged or lost, we will ask you to replace it for the price of $50.00. We appreciate your cooperation.

Cinemata Video

Forty-seventh Street Store

31. Why was this letter sent?
  (A) The man has won a DVD.
  (B) The man's check was no good.
  (C) The man must pay $5.00.
  (D) The man's lost case has been found.

32. What should the man do?
  (A) Look for his friend, Linda
  (B) Come to the movie theater
  (C) Return a DVD with a payment
  (D) Join the cooperative

33. What happened on July 17?
  (A) Mr. Nunn met Linda.
  (B) Mr. Nunn checked out an item.
  (C) Mr. Nunn missed work.
  (D) The store started its business.

●仮定法

A. まずは次の基本形を覚えておきましょう。助動詞の過去形が出てきたら、仮定法ではないか疑ってみましょう。

●仮定法過去

If S 過去形…, S would [should / could / might] 原形 …

例：If I *knew* his phone number, I could contact him at once.

（彼の電話番号がわかっていれば、すぐに連絡がとれるのだが）

●仮定法過去完了

If S had 過去分詞…, S would [should / could / might] have 過去分詞…

例：If I *had known* his phone number then, I could have contacted him at once.

（その時彼の電話番号がわかっていれば、すぐに連絡をとれたのだが）

B. ifを用いない代わりに、以下の部分を倒置することもあります。

例：*Were it* (＝ If it were) not for water, we could not live.

（水がなければ、私たちは生きられない）

例：*Should there* (＝ If there should) be any errors in this draft, please call me at extension 11.

（万一この草稿に何らかの誤りがございましたら、内線11までお電話ください）

・・・

学習のヒント

　パート3や4では、「この対話／文章の話題は何か」（【Unit 1 問9】、【Unit 5 問8】／【Unit 3 問12】、【Unit 5 問13】など）や「どこでの対話／文章か」（【Unit 2 問9】、【Unit 4 問10】／【Unit 1 問12】、【Unit 2 問12】など）がよく問われます。こういった問題は、対話や文章のおおよその内容が理解できれば答えることができ、必ず正解すべきものです。特に入門レベルの学習者では、細かいところまで聞きのがすまいとするあまり、かえって全体が見えなくなる場合があります。パート3と4では、まず、全体のおおよその内容を理解することを意識して練習してみてください。

　練習していくうちに細部も注意して聴きとる余裕が出てきたら、特に「年月や日時や曜日」、「場所」、「数値」といった情報に耳をそばだててください。パート3や4では、こういった情報についての設問もよくあります。

・・・

Unit 5

●●● Warm-up & Vocabulary Build-up ●●●

英文を聴きとって、空所にあてはまる単語を下の選択肢から選んで入れなさい。

1. An _____ is directing heavy rush-hour traffic.
2. A car has pulled off the road onto the _____.
3. The bridge can be seen in the _____.
4. Is the party for a special _____?
5. My _____ is importing foreign cars.
6. Corn is the main _____ grown in this region.
7. Everyone must _____ at the hotel on the first day.
8. The company _____ its monthly sales report.

a. crop	**b.** distance	**c.** occasion	**d.** occupation
e. officer	**f.** register	**g.** released	**h.** shoulder

Part 1 **Photographs**

You will hear four short statements. Look at the picture, and select the statement that best describes what you see in the picture.

1.

(A)　(B)　(C)　(D)

2.

(A)　(B)　(C)　(D)

Part 2　Question-Response

You will hear a question or statement and three responses. Listen carefully, and select the best response to the question or statement.

3.　(A)　(B)　(C)

4.　(A)　(B)　(C)

5.　(A)　(B)　(C)

6.　(A)　(B)　(C)

7.　(A)　(B)　(C)

Part 3 — Conversations

You will hear a short conversation between two people. Listen carefully, and select the best response to each question.

8. What is this discussion about?
- (A) Not receiving the paper
- (B) Canceling a subscription
- (C) The rates for placing an ad
- (D) The cost for home delivery

9. What will the employees receive?
- (A) Printed copies of their records
- (B) New identification cards
- (C) Cases for carrying documents
- (D) New business cards

10. How long will he live in St. Louis?
- (A) Ten days
- (B) Two weeks
- (C) A half year
- (D) Two years

11. What is the man looking for?
- (A) A new house
- (B) An apartment
- (C) A condominium
- (D) A real estate agent

Part 4 — Talks

You will hear a short talk given by a single speaker. Listen carefully, and select the best response to each question.

12. What mistake has this person made?
- (A) He had too many carry-ons.
- (B) He took the wrong plane.
- (C) He left a bag behind.
- (D) His bag had no tag.

13. What is this announcement about?
- (A) A woman has won a bike.
- (B) The park is closing.
- (C) Parking is not allowed here.
- (D) A lost animal has been found.

14. What are they scheduled to do now?
- (A) Go skiing
- (B) Go ice climbing
- (C) Eat lunch
- (D) See glaciers

📖 READING

●●● Vocabulary Build-up ●●●

空所にあてはまる単語を、下の選択肢から選んで入れなさい。

1. Many different _____ came to their wedding.
2. The museum is showing regional _____ art.
3. There are several _____ through these woods.
4. Tickets for the play are still _____.
5. Businesses come to the university to _____ employees.
6. This small project has a narrow _____.
7. We are _____ for all of your help.
8. _____ outside on our patio.

a. available	**b.** dine	**c.** folk	**d.** grateful
e. recruit	**f.** relatives	**g.** scope	**h.** trails

Part 5 — Incomplete Sentences

A word or phrase is missing in each of the sentences. Select the best answer to complete each sentence.

15. Linda has decided _____ her necklace.
  (A) sold
  (B) selling
  (C) to sell
  (D) sells

16. The teacher told us _____.
  (A) be quiet
  (B) to be quiet
  (C) quiet
  (D) being quiet

17. What would you like us _____ for the class on sports day?
  (A) do
  (B) to do
  (C) done
  (D) doing

18. _____ the life of the car's engine, the oil should be changed often.
  (A) Extending
  (B) To extend
  (C) The extending
  (D) Extends

19. Dr. Williams would always make his students _____ a speech on the last day.
  (A) to give
  (B) give
  (C) giving
  (D) given

20. _____ water on the fire at the campsite to put it out.

    (A) Take   (B) Give

    (C) Add   (D) Pour

21. Are you happy with how everything is _____?

    (A) taking   (B) finding

    (C) sorting   (D) going

22. Who _____ the musician to play the piano so well?

    (A) scheduled   (B) allowed

    (C) taught   (D) suggested

23. She _____ on the couch when she began to feel sick.

    (A) went   (B) lay

    (C) lied   (D) carried

24. The post office is just across the bridge, _____ to the coffee shop.

    (A) past   (B) at the back

    (C) around   (D) next

Part 6 — Text Completion

Read the text that follows. A word, phrase, or sentence is missing in parts of the text. Select the best answer to complete the text.

● Questions 25-28 refer to the following advertisement.

Looking for a Sports Editor

As sports editor, you would supervise the copy desk, _____ story writing, and
25.

give your ideas for the direction of our newspaper's sports section. _____. As a
26.

manager, you would also rate the performance of people in _____ department.
27.

You would also need to have strong editing skills and a deep understanding of

_____.
28.

---

25. (A) check
(B) checked
(C) checking
(D) to check

26. (A) Our paper is sold every weekday for $1.50 and the weekend edition sells for $2.00.
(B) Please tell us if you have any problems with your new video game and we will help you.
(C) Yesterday the Eagles beat the Crows in an exciting game that ended in overtime play.
(D) Your job would include working with other reporters on stories and meeting deadlines.

27. (A) their
(B) they
(C) you
(D) your

28. (A) business
(B) government
(C) sports
(D) weather

Read the following selection of texts. Select the best answer for each question.

●Questions 29-30 refer to the following notice.

Water Use Policy

Regulations to limit water use require the following changes in company policy.

Do not give customers water or refill their glasses unless they ask for it. Never start the dishwasher unless it is full. Turn on the water only to fill containers. Do not wash vegetables under running water. Reuse water from the sink to wash the floor. Do not flush the toilet unnecessarily or wash your hands under running water.

29. Where is this notice found?
  (A) At a swimming pool
  (B) At a restaurant
  (C) At a supermarket
  (D) At a carwash

30. Which of the following is permitted?
  (A) Giving out unrequested water
  (B) Cleaning vegetables under running water
  (C) Washing dishes by machine
  (D) Washing floors with clean water

●Questions 31-33 refer to the following statement.

Here are the sales figures for the second quarter:

Store	April	May	June	Entire Quarter
Carpenter	103.1	110.6	112.0	108.6
Downtown*	98.6	94.3	99.3	97.4
Princeton	109.7	121.8	135.7	122.4
Westside	184.9	223.6	236.9	215.1

100 = average sales month at that branch during the previous year
*Closed July 1 for the entire third quarter.

31. Which store had a slight recovery in June?
  (A) Carpenter
  (B) Princeton
  (C) Downtown
  (D) Westside

32. What is the overall trend?
  (A) Sales are increasing.
  (B) All stores have slight drops.
  (C) Sales have doubled everywhere.
  (D) Three stores are behind last year.

33. What will happen at the downtown store?
  (A) Its sales may improve in July.
  (B) It should outsell all stores in July.
  (C) It will open fifteen minutes later.
  (D) It will reopen about October 1.

文法チェック ✔

●準動詞（１）

A. to不定詞（to do）と動名詞（〜ing）は、名詞の働きをすることができますから、文の中で主語、補語、目的語になることができます。

B. to不定詞は、副詞の働きができますから、動詞などの修飾要素になることができます。

例：He went abroad *to study* art.
　　（彼は芸術を勉強するために外国に行った）［目的］

例：I was surprised *to see* you in a place like that.
　　（あんなところであなたを見かけて驚いた）［感情の原因］

例：He grew up *to be* a good doctor.
　　（彼は成長して立派な医者になった）［結果］

C. 原形不定詞（動詞の原形）は、使役動詞（make、have）や知覚動詞（see、hearなど）の補語になることができます。

学習のヒント

　パート3や4では、パート1や2と比べ、聴きとるべき英語の量が格段に多くなります。全体のおおよその内容を理解できるようにする、余裕が出てきたら細部もできるだけ聴きとることができるようにする、と進んだら、最終的には、全体としてネイティブ・スピーカーが話す速度（150〜200語／分）についていけるようにしましょう。いちいち和訳していては、この速度にはついていけません。できるだけ英語のまま理解できるよう、意識して何度も聴いて練習してみましょう。

　英語のまま直接理解するためには、流れてくる英語を意味のかたまりごとに処理していかなければなりません。英語では語順が決まっていますから、たとえば、「誰が」（主語の部分）、「何をしたのか」（動詞の部分）、「どのように」、「どこで」、「いつ」、といったぐあいに、流れてくる英語をその順番どおりに処理していくことが必要です。そのためには、かたまりになっているところを正確に理解する必要があります。たとえば、The man / who / is fishing / in the pond / is my father. という文は、「/」のところで区切ることができます。この文ではかたまりの最初に現れるのがwho（関係代名詞）やin（前置詞）などですが、このほかにもいろいろな場合があります。つまり、リスニングであっても、文法的な知識がある程度必要ということです。文法というと敬遠されがちですが、高度な知識は必要ありませんので、基本的なところを充実させておきましょう。こういった知識は、パート5をはじめとしたリーディング・セクションでも大いに活かされるはずです。

Unit 6

 **LISTENING**

●●● Warm-up & Vocabulary Build-up ●●●

英文を聴きとって、空所にあてはまる単語を下の選択肢から選んで入れなさい。

1. The musicians are taking a _____ on the stage.
2. The _____ has large fields of wheat.
3. Did you _____ the last train?
4. Did you have enough time to _____ the test?
5. Do the farmers expect a good _____ this year?
6. Follow these _____ to our hotel.
7. There is a charge for extra _____.
8. This bus stops at the college's new sports _____.

| **a.** baggage | **b.** bow | **c.** complete | **d.** directions |
| **e.** facilities | **f.** farm | **g.** harvest | **h.** miss |

Part 1 **Photographs**

You will hear four short statements. Look at the picture, and select the statement that best describes what you see in the picture.

1.

(A) (B) (C) (D)

2.

(A) (B) (C) (D)

Part 2 Question-Response

You will hear a question or statement and three responses. Listen carefully, and select the best response to the question or statement.

3. (A) (B) (C)

4. (A) (B) (C)

5. (A) (B) (C)

6. (A) (B) (C)

7. (A) (B) (C)

Part 3 — Conversations

You will hear a short conversation between two people. Listen carefully, and select the best response to each question.

8. What is the man doing?
    (A) Visiting his dentist
    (B) Trying on new hats
    (C) Showing a friend his town
    (D) Hiring a temporary assistant

9. What is wrong with the coat?
    (A) It is too small.
    (B) It is too expensive.
    (C) It is the wrong style.
    (D) The color is wrong.

10. What are they discussing?
    (A) Looking for a job
    (B) Hiring a new employee
    (C) Creating a new position
    (D) Working for an agency

11. What seems to be the problem?
    (A) She cannot find her receipt.
    (B) They do not have her size.
    (C) The blouse no longer fits.
    (D) She has two matching blouses.

Part 4 — Talks

You will hear a short talk given by a single speaker. Listen carefully, and select the best response to each question.

12. What is the point of this announcement?
    (A) To make drivers slow down
    (B) To protect children
    (C) To sell cars
    (D) To get cars locked up

13. What do these instructions explain?
    (A) Operating a photocopier
    (B) Buying a newspaper from a vending box
    (C) Putting up wallpaper
    (D) Washing clothes by hand

14. What should the caller do to leave a phone number?
    (A) Press the star key
    (B) Press the pound key
    (C) Wait for the beep
    (D) Dial again

📖 READING

●● ⦁ Vocabulary Build-up ⦁ ●●

空所にあてはまる単語を、下の選択肢から選んで入れなさい。

1. The stores always close at 5:00 _____.
2. Nancy was _____ to run her department.
3. He _____ that he would run for mayor.
4. Tim was _____ to know that his illness was not serious.
5. The company's _____ price rose again today.
6. These baking directions must be followed _____.
7. The lecture will be about the recent growth in regional _____.
8. The factory closed after _____ costs jumped greatly.

a. commerce	**b.** declared	**c.** labor	**d.** promoted
e. relieved	**f.** sharp	**g.** stock	**h.** strictly

Part 5 / Incomplete Sentences /

A word or phrase is missing in each of the sentences. Select the best answer to complete each sentence.

15. Don't forget _____ me a postcard when you're on vacation.
    - (A) send
    - (B) sending
    - (C) will send
    - (D) to send

16. Could you _____ to finish your work before the deadline?
    - (A) do
    - (B) manage
    - (C) complete
    - (D) achieve

17. Jina went abroad _____ last month.
    - (A) study
    - (B) studying
    - (C) to study
    - (D) studied

18. Bill had his sister _____ the living room.
    - (A) clean
    - (B) cleans
    - (C) to clean
    - (D) cleaned

19. The last period of the day is scheduled _____ 3:00.
    - (A) start for
    - (B) from the start
    - (C) to start at
    - (D) starting with

20. The state did not _____ motorcycle riders to wear helmets until five years ago.

    (A) require   (B) acquire

    (C) resign   (D) inquire

21. The applicant is well _____ for the job.

    (A) classified   (B) limited

    (C) characterized   (D) qualified

22. The order should _____ within the next two days.

    (A) arrive   (B) send

    (C) carry   (D) stay

23. If you want to return a purchase, you _____ have a receipt.

    (A) want   (B) require

    (C) get   (D) must

24. Julie usually runs _____ the jogging trail every morning before going to work.

    (A) on   (B) into

    (C) with   (D) where

Part 6 Text Completion

Read the text that follows. A word, phrase, or sentence is missing in parts of the text. Select the best answer to complete the text.

●Questions 25-28 refer to the following job advertisement.

Help Wanted

Helpful Hardware Store is _____ for hard-working, friendly employees. We
        25.

need people who have experience in one of the following areas: Painting, Building,

or Lighting. We _____ need people who have had previous jobs as cashiers
       26.

and shelf stockers. _____. We offer great benefits, including health care, life
       27.

insurance, and a retirement _____.
       28.

25. (A) finding
    (B) hosting
    (C) looking
    (D) reaching

26. (A) already
    (B) also
    (C) never
    (D) yet

27. (A) If you have experience in any of these areas, please apply in person at our store.
    (B) The people who fill out our survey will receive a free bag with our logo on it.
    (C) The store will be closing for good next week and we have many items on sale.
    (D) You can make your own mug and bowl in our craft corner, so come in soon.

28. (A) future
    (B) garden
    (C) plan
    (D) sport

Read the following selection of texts. Select the best answer for each question.

● Questions 29-31 refer to the following schedule.

Air Ste. Lawrence flights into Quebec City

From	Arriving at	Frequency
Boston	11:30 A.M., 2:45 & 5:00 P.M.	daily, no 5:00 flight on weekends
Toronto	9:30 & 11:00 A.M., 1:30, 4:00 & 7:30 P.M.	also 9:00 on Fridays
Ottawa	10:15 A.M., 5:45 P.M.	daily
New York	12:00 noon, 2:00, 6:00 & 8:30 P.M.	also 10:00 Fridays and Saturdays

29. Where does the earliest flight come from?
    (A) Boston
    (B) Toronto
    (C) Ottawa
    (D) New York

30. When do four flights arrive from New York?
    (A) Every day
    (B) Five days a week
    (C) On Fridays
    (D) On weekends

31. Which city has no changes in its schedule?
    (A) Ottawa
    (B) Boston
    (C) New York
    (D) Quebec City

●Questions 32-34 refer to the following text message chain.

Julian Marks [14:44]
Hi, Amanda. I'm about to go into the meeting with Miller and Associates, but I forgot the flash drive on my desk.
Can you send me one file from it?

Amanda Price [14:46]
No problem. I'm in your office now and I see the flash drive. Which file do you need?

Julian Marks [14:46]
It's the spreadsheet labeled 'June 10 report.' Could you e-mail it to me?

Amanda Price [14:49]
There. All done.

Julian Marks [14:51]
Got it. Now I can open it on my laptop and refer to it during the meeting. Thanks a million.

Amanda Price [14:51]
Of course. Good luck!

32. What does Mr. Marks ask Ms. Price to do?
(A) Call some clients
(B) Reschedule a meeting
(C) Send some data
(D) Take over a presentation

33. At 14:46, what does Ms. Price mean when she says, "No problem"?
(A) She agrees to Mr. Marks's request.
(B) She found the file easily.
(C) She has solved a problem.
(D) She no longer works with Mr. Marks.

34. What will Mr. Marks do soon?
(A) Leave his office
(B) Meet with Ms. Marks
(C) Take a break
(D) Talk about a report

●準動詞 (2)

A. to不定詞や動名詞が動詞の目的語になるときには、どちらなのかによって意味が異なることがあります。

例：I remember *seeing* him somewhere.

（私はどこかで彼に<u>会った</u>覚えがある）

例：You should remember *to see* him this afternoon.

（今日の午後彼に<u>会う</u>のを覚えておいてくださいね）

B. 準動詞のうち、SVOCのCとしてもっともよく使われるのはto不定詞です。Cとして原形不定詞や分詞が使われるのは、Vが使役動詞や知覚動詞など限られた場合ですから、こちらの方をしっかり覚えておきましょう。

• •

学習のヒント

　聴くことと読むことの間には密接な関係があると言われています。読んで理解することができないのに、聴いて理解することなどできません。リスニングの力を向上させるためにも、早く読む練習をしましょう。ポイントは、ユニット5の「学習のヒント」で触れた、リスニングの場合と同じです。英文を左から右へ、意味のかたまりごとに理解していけるよう意識して練習してみましょう。これは、パート6や7に対する対策にもなります。

　また、聴くことと話すことの間にも密接な関係があると言われています。正しく、自然な発音を自分ですることができない単語や文を正確に聴きとることはできません。ストリーミング音声を使って、耳から聞こえてきた英語を何度も口に出して自分で言ってみましょう。教員からスクリプトが配布されているのなら、それを見ながら聴いてみるのもよい練習になります。文字を目で追いながら、音声に耳を傾けてみてください。さらに、同時に口に出してみるのも、つまり、「耳と目と口を連動させて」練習するのも、リスニングの力を向上させる上で有効な方法です。入門レベルの学習者にとって重要なのは、何度も聴くことによって（それも、いろいろな方法で）、まずは耳を英語に慣らすことです。繰り返しの練習が大切です。

• •

Unit 7

 LISTENING 36

●●○ **Warm-up & Vocabulary Build-up** ○●●

英文を聴きとって、空所にあてはまる単語を下の選択肢から選んで入れなさい。

1. The man is _____ against the wall.
2. Small music players have the _____ to be top sellers.
3. Will you _____ the meeting this afternoon?
4. Did you _____ that our car is almost out of gas?
5. The area has a _____ of power during the summer months.
6. She _____ the speech with her personal thoughts.
7. Please _____ to the building's entrance.
8. _____ at the company is rather formal.

a. attend	**b.** attire	**c.** concluded	**d.** lack
e. leaning	**f.** potential	**g.** proceed	**h.** realize

| **Part 1** | **Photographs** | 37 |

You will hear four short statements. Look at the picture, and select the statement that best describes what you see in the picture.

1.

(A) (B) (C) (D)

2.

(A)   (B)   (C)   (D)

Part 2 Question-Response

You will hear a question or statement and three responses. Listen carefully, and select the best response to the question or statement.

3. (A) (B) (C)

4. (A) (B) (C)

5. (A) (B) (C)

6. (A) (B) (C)

7. (A) (B) (C)

You will hear a short conversation between two people. Listen carefully, and select the best response to each question.

8. Why is the man worried about the hotel?
   (A) Last year, he could not get a room.
   (B) He stayed in a bad hotel before.
   (C) The pictures do not look good.
   (D) He stayed in the hotel last year.

9. What did the woman notice?
   (A) The different shape of eyeglasses
   (B) A new picture frame
   (C) His new hair color
   (D) The man's darker frames

10. How was this workshop different from the previous one?
   (A) People spent less time.
   (B) The turnout of people was 15 percent less.
   (C) Costs were held down.
   (D) More money was spent this time.

11. What will the company do soon?
   (A) Go back to their old logo
   (B) Close for a week
   (C) Search for a new logo
   (D) Buy supplies with a new logo

Part 4 — Talks

You will hear a short talk given by a single speaker. Listen carefully, and select the best response to each question.

12. Why did Jane make this call?
   (A) To apologize   (B) To repair her car
   (C) To wake up Mr. Longman   (D) To ask something

13. What are the directions for?
   (A) Pressing clothing   (B) Removing a stain
   (C) Operating a washer   (D) Dyeing clothes

14. What is being requested?
   (A) To leave a message   (B) To call back later
   (C) To wait a moment   (D) To answer the phone

📖 READING

●●● Vocabulary Build-up ●●●

空所にあてはまる単語を、下の選択肢から選んで入れなさい。

1. The celebration will _____ a fireworks display.
2. The group thanked her for her years of _____.
3. Sheila's language skills _____ the company executives.
4. This law _____ the cost of using credit cards.
5. Charges on the _____ should be paid by Friday.
6. Many old newspapers had _____ in the garage.
7. All of the bank's _____ are now open on Saturdays.
8. Our company takes an _____ role in helping others.

a. accumulated	**b.** active	**c.** branches	**d.** concerns
e. impressed	**f.** include	**g.** invoice	**h.** involvement

Part 5 　Incomplete Sentences

A word or phrase is missing in each of the sentences. Select the best answer to complete each sentence.

15. Thank you for _____ me organize the meeting.
- (A) helping
- (B) help
- (C) helped
- (D) to help

16. Have you finished _____ your room?
- (A) clean
- (B) to clean
- (C) cleaning
- (D) cleaned

17. The movie was very _____.
- (A) bored
- (B) boring
- (C) excited
- (D) slowly

18. Drivers must follow the directions _____ on street signs.
- (A) written
- (B) writing
- (C) write
- (D) wrote

19. The president told Linda Lynn that she would have an executive position, _____ was highly doubtful to her.
- (A) where
- (B) which
- (C) who
- (D) whose

20. Betty read the _____ carefully before she began working.

    (A) instructed   (B) instructor

    (C) instruct   (D) instructions

21. It is really a beautiful home, but the _____ is too high for my family to buy.

    (A) expenses   (B) money

    (C) price   (D) value

22. What was the boss's _____ to your suggestion?

    (A) review   (B) react

    (C) response   (D) opinion

23. The shopper did not know the bags of _____ were not her own.

    (A) diet   (B) menu

    (C) groceries   (D) crops

24. After careful consideration, Gregg Hunt _____ decided to enroll in the Effective Management Practices program.

    (A) closely   (B) eventually

    (C) exceptionally   (D) highly

Part 6 Text Completion

Read the text that follows. A word, phrase, or sentence is missing in parts of the text. Select the best answer to complete the text.

● Questions 25-28 refer to the following letter.

Dear Mr. Nagle,

Thank you again for taking the time to _____ with me about your company's
                                              25.

job openings. _____. I would like to confirm that I am very _____ in
                  26.   **27.**

working for your company. I would be willing to do any job that you might be able

to offer at this time. I look forward to hearing _____ you.
                                                      28.

Sincerely,

Brian Jones

25. (A) ask
　　　 (B) help
　　　 (C) meet
　　　 (D) stay

26. (A) I enjoyed talking with you and learning more about Endbrink's goals and
　　　　　products.
　　　 (B) I hope your company will consider my proposal about a joint project with
　　　　　my firm.
　　　 (C) If you ever need a reference for a future job position, I would be happy to
　　　　　supply one.
　　　 (D) I'm very sorry to say I cannot make the interview that we scheduled for
　　　　　tomorrow.

27. (A) interest
　　　 (B) interested
　　　 (C) interesting
　　　 (D) interestingly

28. (A) about
　　　 (B) for
　　　 (C) from
　　　 (D) to

Read the following selection of texts. Select the best answer for each question.

●Questions 29-31 refer to the following vacation plan.

Hotel Kenilworth-Bristol, England:-----------------------------$110 for a double
> Excellent location, includes breakfast.
> Stay in a building over 200 years old!

Schwartzenkopp Garden-Hannover, Germany:-------$90, singles only
> Quiet, long-term rental available.
> Just one minute from the subway and neighborhood shops.

Hotel Wailua-Kauai Island, Hawaii:-------------------------- $200 for a twin
> Enjoy tropical beaches.
> Drive to Wailua Falls.

Mount Denali Lodge-Cantwell, Alaska:------------------$170 for a double
> Breathtaking mountain views.
> Ask about our discount fishing excursion.

---

29. Which hotel can be rented on a weekly basis?
    (A) Schwartzenkopp Garden
    (B) Mount Denali Lodge
    (C) The hotel near the waterfall
    (D) The hotel in Bristol

30. Which hotel is the cheapest for two people?
    (A) The hotel near the subway
    (B) The hotel with the fishing plan
    (C) The hotel in Germany
    (D) The English hotel

31. How much does the historic hotel cost?
    (A) $90
    (B) $100
    (C) $110
    (D) $170

●Questions 32-34 refer to the following webpage.

← Free Seminar Assesses Your Computer Skills ➡

* Have you always wanted to learn about computers?
* Do you know a little about computers and want to learn more?
* Are you unsure what courses would be best for you to take?

Two free computer orientation seminars are being offered to help you decide what computer courses you should take. The information sessions will be held on Tuesday, January 5 from 5:30 to 6:30 P.M. and on Saturday, January 9 from 10:00 to 11:00 A.M. Instructors will be available to answer your questions and provide one-on-one consultation and advice. They'll also be able to register you immediately in the computer courses of your choice.

32. What is mentioned about the seminar?
- (A) Advanced registration is required.
- (B) Attendees do not have to pay for it.
- (C) It is held on only one day.
- (D) It is only for computer beginners.

33. How long does each seminar last?
- (A) One hour
- (B) Two hours
- (C) Two days
- (D) A few weeks

34. What is the purpose of the seminar?
- (A) To find out who already knows about computers
- (B) To find out who would make a good computer teacher
- (C) To help determine which computer classes to take
- (D) To learn as much as possible about computers

文法チェック ✔

●準動詞（3）

A. to不定詞と動名詞のうち、前置詞の目的語になる（前置詞の後に続ける）ことができるのは、動名詞だけです。

B. to不定詞や動名詞が動詞の目的語になるときには、使い分けが必要になることがあります。動名詞を目的語とする動詞は限られていますから、こちらをしっかり覚えておきましょう。avoid、enjoy、finish、mind、quit、stopなどです。

C. 分詞には現在分詞と過去分詞があります。現在分詞は「〜する」（能動）、「〜している」（進行）の意味です。過去分詞は、他動詞の場合「〜される」（受け身）と自動詞の場合「〜してしまった」（完了）で意味が異なります。なお、動名詞と現在分詞は同じ形ですから、文中での位置や働きからしっかりと区別してください。

D. 現在分詞と過去分詞では、表す意味が異なりますから、意味に応じた使い分けが大切です。特に注意したいのは、もとになる動詞の意味が「〜させる」の場合です。たとえば、exciteは「興奮する」ではなく「興奮させる」という意味です。ですから、「彼は興奮している」と言いたいときは、He is exciting. ではなく、He is excited.（彼は興奮させられている）になります。

E. 分詞は、形容詞の働きができますから、補語や名詞の修飾要素になることができます。名詞の修飾要素となるときは、単独ならその名詞の前に、他の語句と一緒に語群になっているならその名詞の後に、それぞれ置かれます。

学習のヒント

　パート2と3では、対話が素材になっています。それも、日常生活のいろいろな場面や、さまざまなビジネスシーンなど、幅広い場面が想定されています。そういった場面で典型的に用いられる表現を、できるだけたくさん身につけましょう。これはTOEIC®でよいスコアをとる上でも大いに役立ちますが、実生活にも当然活かすことができる知識です。このテキストを使う授業のそもそもの目的はTOEIC® Listening & Reading Test対策であることが多いとは思いますが、それだけで終わらせてしまっては少々もったいない気がします。せっかく苦労して身につけた知識ですから、幅広く活かすことができれば、それに越したことはありません。TOEIC®対策をTOEIC®対策だけに終わらせず、パート2と3については、ぜひ一種の「英会話例文集」としても活用してみてください。

Unit 8

🎧 LISTENING

●●● **Warm-up & Vocabulary Build-up** ●●●

英文を聴きとって、空所にあてはまる単語を下の選択肢から選んで入れなさい。

1. Can anyone _____ this Korean message into English?
2. Wood chips are _____ over the ground.
3. During August, the building will _____ its lobby.
4. Some farms _____ from poor vegetable crops.
5. Our _____ library has lots of videos.
6. A long walkway _____ Terminals C and D.
7. The luggage is being _____ onto the bus.
8. The express train _____ from Track 5.

a. connects	**b.** departs	**c.** loaded	**d.** public
e. renovate	**f.** scattered	**g.** suffer	**h.** translate

Part 1 **Photographs**

You will hear four short statements. Look at the picture, and select the statement that best describes what you see in the picture.

1.

(A) (B) (C) (D)

2.

(A) (B) (C) (D)

Part 2 Question-Response

You will hear a question or statement and three responses. Listen carefully, and select the best response to the question or statement.

3. (A) (B) (C)

4. (A) (B) (C)

5. (A) (B) (C)

6. (A) (B) (C)

7. (A) (B) (C)

You will hear a short conversation between two people. Listen carefully, and select the best response to each question.

8. What does the woman think of the schedule?
    - (A) Her second job runs too late.
    - (B) All the good jobs have been taken.
    - (C) Everyone could work more.
    - (D) It is too tiring for her.

9. What are these people preparing to do?
    - (A) Go to work by train
    - (B) Have their carry-on checked
    - (C) Get a taxi
    - (D) Load the man's car

10. What is the man asking about?
    - (A) When the class will be over
    - (B) Why the woman will be working late
    - (C) If the woman needs a ride home
    - (D) Where the man should pick her up

11. What are they discussing?
    - (A) Needing stronger glasses
    - (B) Buying some glassware
    - (C) Finding something to read
    - (D) A misplaced personal item

You will hear a short talk given by a single speaker. Listen carefully, and select the best response to each question.

12. When is there a five-dollar charge?
    - (A) When payment is late
    - (B) If you cancel the purchase
    - (C) When shipping is needed
    - (D) On the 15th of each month

13. How will the weather in the eastern area be?
    - (A) Cloudy
    - (B) Hot
    - (C) Mild
    - (D) Rainy

14. What will happen tomorrow afternoon?
    - (A) It will be colder.
    - (B) There will be snow.
    - (C) It will rain.
    - (D) The sky will clear up.

📖 READING

●●● Vocabulary Build-up ●●●

空所にあてはまる単語を、下の選択肢から選んで入れなさい。

1. It has taken over a _____ to write this book.
2. Newspapers are delivered to homes before _____ .
3. Liz was so tired that she _____ on the couch.
4. Our school will help you toward a _____ in nursing.
5. This _____ is used to reduce pain.
6. The operation of this machine _____ special training.
7. We have an _____ selection of fine jewelry.
8. After Betty recovered from her cold, her _____ condition started to improve.

a. collapsed	**b.** career	**c.** dawn	**d.** decade
e. extensive	**f.** medicine	**g.** physical	**h.** requires

Part 5　Incomplete Sentences

A word or phrase is missing in each of the sentences. Select the best answer to complete each sentence.

15. _____ there was little evidence indicating a risk of infection, the panel concluded that no additional measures were needed.
    - (A) Although
    - (B) If
    - (C) Since
    - (D) Unless

16. Because of the _____ waves, all boats must be kept tied up.
    - (A) raising
    - (B) rising
    - (C) risen
    - (D) raised

17. I saw Lucy _____ for a bus.
    - (A) waits
    - (B) to wait
    - (C) waiting
    - (D) waited

18. The lights went out suddenly, _____ everyone in the room.
    - (A) in surprise
    - (B) surprising
    - (C) surprisingly
    - (D) surprised

19. The supervisor always tells his workers that when _____ clients, enjoying the time together and not forcing business transactions are crucial.

    (A) entertain   (B) entertained

    (C) entertaining   (D) entertains

20. Students should wait at the _____ to the school.

    (A) entrance   (B) enter

    (C) entering   (D) enterable

21. If you don't have a _____ on weekends, you would not be able to stay at our hotel.

    (A) reservation   (B) reservist

    (C) reserve   (D) reservoir

22. _____ agrees that Mayor Smith should be re-elected.

    (A) Not everyone   (B) Every other

    (C) Not even   (D) Everyone does not

23. This workshop will be useful to _____ whose career goal is to run a successful business.

    (A) anyone   (B) one another

    (C) others   (D) whoever

24. The shelf above the desk is filled _____ books.

    (A) with   (B) of

    (C) from   (D) to

Part 6   Text Completion

Read the text that follows. A word, phrase, or sentence is missing in parts of the text. Select the best answer to complete the text.

● Questions 25-28 refer to the following announcement.

The Travel Show _____, Friday, Saturday, and Sunday, April 17, 18, and
                              25.
19. This is an _____ three-day travel information show for the leisure or
                          26.
business traveler. In addition to visiting over 100 exhibitor booths, you can

_____ video travelogues, live cultural dances, and music demonstrations.
   27.
There will also be drawings and over 50 vacation door prizes. _____.
                                                                       28.

---

25. (A) holds
　　 (B) was hold
　　 (C) will be held
　　 (D) will hold

26. (A) excitable
　　 (B) excitably
　　 (C) excite
　　 (D) exciting

27. (A) collect
　　 (B) have
　　 (C) make
　　 (D) watch

28. (A) A fun weekend getaway is just what you may need.
　　 (B) Tickets are completely sold out for this popular movie.
　　 (C) Tickets may be purchased for $6.00 each at the door.
　　 (D) You should make a reservation to dine with us soon.

Read the following selection of texts. Select the best answer for each question.

● Questions 29-31 refer to the following information.

MEDICAL INSURANCE COVERAGE

Routine Medical Expenses:

After a $500 deductible, the plan pays 80% of the next $1,000, and 50% of the remaining expenses. Prescriptions not included.

Surgical Expenses:

The plan pays the first $1,000 of expenses in full, and 50% of remaining expenses. Does not include oral surgery.

29. If medical expenses are $500, how much does the plan pay?
- (A) Nothing
- (B) $250
- (C) $400
- (D) $500

30. What is the out-of-pocket expense for an operation costing $1,500?
- (A) $200
- (B) $250
- (C) $700
- (D) $1,250

31. Which of the following would be covered most completely by the insurance?
- (A) Medication
- (B) Gum surgery
- (C) A regular check-up
- (D) A non-emergency operation

● Questions 32-34 refer to the following online discussion.

Kelly Simms [16:30] Jacob and Marcy, do you have a minute? I just wanted to ask how your new employee, Isabel Lorde, is doing.

Marcy Collins [16:31] Oh, excellent. She is very quick to learn and keen to try new things.

Kelly Simms [16:32] Excellent. We're going to promote our healthy drinks at local schools, and I need someone to work with the marketing department on merchandise and posters that would appeal to young people.

Jacob Phelps [16:37] I'm sure she would be great. How much time will this take? We do still need her on the Williams account.

Kelly Simms [16:38] How about mornings only for three days next week?

Marcy Collins [16:39] Sounds good to me. We'll be done with the Williams account by the end of this week, right, Jacob?

Jacob Phelps [16:39] It will be tight, but I think so.

Kelly Simms [16:41] Great. Thanks to you both. I'll talk to Isabel on Friday.

32. What are the employees discussing?
- (A) A local school
- (B) A new employee
- (C) A successful campaign
- (D) An important meeting

33. At 16:39, what does Mr. Phelps mean when he says, "It will be tight"?
- (A) He cannot fit everything in his office.
- (B) He is uncomfortable with the plan.
- (C) He thinks the deadline will be close.
- (D) He wants to think about the proposal more.

34. What will Ms. Lorde be asked to do next week?
- (A) Be Ms. Simms's assistant
- (B) Continue on the Williams account
- (C) Train a new employee
- (D) Work with the marketing department

●準動詞（4）

A. 分詞は、使役動詞（make、have、get）や知覚動詞（see、hearなど）の補語になることができます。ここでも、現在分詞と過去分詞の意味の違いが重要です。表すべき意味を、その前にある名詞との関係で考えてみてください。次の例では、「私の部屋」が赤く「塗られる」という受け身の関係ですから、過去分詞が用いられています。

例：I had my room *painted* red.

（私は部屋を赤く塗ってもらった）

B. 分詞は、副詞節と同じ働きをする表現をつくることができます。このような表現を「分詞構文」と言っていますが、文頭、主語と動詞の間または文末のいずれかの位置に現れます。他の部分とのつながりに応じて、さまざまな意味を表すことができます。

例：*Being tired* (=Because I was tired), I decided to take a rest for a while.

（疲れたので、短時間休憩をとることにした）［理由］

例：He left the place, *waving his right hand*.

（彼は右手を振りながらその場を立ち去った）［付帯状況］

C. 分詞構文でも、現在分詞と過去分詞の使い分けが重要です。分詞構文の主語（省略されているときには主節の主語と同じです）との意味関係を考えてみてください。たとえば、上の2つの例では、「私が疲れている」、「彼が手を振る」といずれも「能動」の意味関係ですから、現在分詞が使われています。一方、次の例では、「ことが考慮される」と「受け身」の意味関係ですから、過去分詞になっています。この例では、分詞構文の中に主語がありますから、この主語との意味関係を考えます。

例：All things *considered*, it is best to do nothing.

（あらゆることを考慮すると、何もしないのが最善だ）

学習のヒント

　TOEIC® Listening & Reading Testのリスニング・セクションでは、各パートの前に、そのパートの説明や例が音声で流されます（パート1の前では、リスニング・セクション全体についての説明も）。ここは聞く必要はありませんから、その時間を利用して、パート1の写真、パート3や4の設問や選択肢をできるだけ見ておきましょう。TOEIC®でよいスコアをとるためには、英語の能力だけでなく、そういった「問題への取り組み方」も実は重要です。このテキストを通して、自分なりの取り組み方も工夫していってみてください。

　リスニング・セクション全体に共通して言えることですが、聞きのがしたりして答が見つからないからといって、いつまでもその問題に固執していては、次の問題への対応まで中途半端になってしまうことになりかねません。とにかくマークして（これも大切なことです）、次の問題に備えましょう（一部聞きのがしたときには「消去法」も有効な方法です）。できれば、問題と問題の間に少しでも余裕をつくって、先へ先へと目を通しておきましょう。何を答えるべきかがわかっていた方が、ずっと解答しやすくなります。

Unit 9

🎧 LISTENING

●●● Warm-up & Vocabulary Build-up ●●●

英文を聴きとって、空所にあてはまる単語を下の選択肢から選んで入れなさい。

1. The driver of the _____ has received a parking ticket.
2. The _____ keeps some of the tables from getting wet.
3. I have _____ pain in my wrists.
4. Can you _____ to have Monday free?
5. Will you show the client to our _____ room?
6. The game will be _____ if the rain continues.
7. The cost of this museum tour includes _____.
8. Using cell phones is not _____ anywhere in this library.

a. admission	**b.** awning	**c.** conference	**d.** manage
e. permitted	**f.** suspended	**g.** terrible	**h.** vehicle

Part 1 　Photographs

You will hear four short statements. Look at the picture, and select the statement that best describes what you see in the picture.

1.

(A)　(B)　(C)　(D)

2.

(A) (B) (C) (D)

Part 2 Question-Response

You will hear a question or statement and three responses. Listen carefully, and select the best response to the question or statement.

3. (A) (B) (C)

4. (A) (B) (C)

5. (A) (B) (C)

6. (A) (B) (C)

7. (A) (B) (C)

You will hear a short conversation between two people. Listen carefully, and select the best response to each question.

8. Why is he going back to school?
- (A) He finds his job boring.
- (B) He wants to be promoted.
- (C) He was fired from this job.
- (D) He has never graduated.

9. What does the woman offer to do?
- (A) Make lunch herself
- (B) Make some phone calls
- (C) Bring the man some lunch
- (D) Have food delivered

10. What time will Mr. Lester most likely come?
- (A) In a few minutes
- (B) The time the man wants
- (C) In time for jogging
- (D) Before the man leaves

11. What will the man plan to do?
- (A) Stay in town tonight
- (B) Spend the night in Rochester
- (C) Use a train and a taxi
- (D) Go the whole way by train

You will hear a short talk given by a single speaker. Listen carefully, and select the best response to each question.

12. How do the customers receive their order?
- (A) By paying by mail
- (B) By visiting the warehouse
- (C) By coming back to the store
- (D) By getting it sent to their home

13. What does a person need to do to get the bag back?
- (A) A description
- (B) Payment in cash
- (C) A receipt
- (D) Identification

14. What is the company seeking?
- (A) An experienced musical actor
- (B) Someone to play a musical instrument
- (C) Someone to conduct the orchestra
- (D) A musician with a recording

📖 READING

●●● Vocabulary Build-up ●●●

空所にあてはまる単語を、下の選択肢から選んで入れなさい。

1. Temperatures are expected to go below _____ tonight.
2. All _____ need to provide their work histories.
3. This _____ report says that most of the work is done.
4. This mill _____ steel for use in buildings.
5. This book has _____ of famous paintings.
6. Customers can get _____ except for certain sale items.
7. Follow these directions to the north _____ of the hospital.
8. Please pay the amount listed at the bottom of this _____.

a. applicants	**b.** bill	**c.** freezing	**d.** produces
e. progress	**f.** refunds	**g.** reproductions	**h.** wing

Part 5　Incomplete Sentences

A word or phrase is missing in each of the sentences. Select the best answer to complete each sentence.

15. The trouble is that we lack _____ materials to complete construction.
    - (A) of remaining
    - (B) our remaining
    - (C) remained
    - (D) the remaining

16. I think it's _____ movie I've ever seen.
    - (A) bad
    - (B) worse
    - (C) the worst
    - (D) much worse

17. The X200 is the _____ of the copiers the company sells now.
    - (A) faster
    - (B) fast
    - (C) fastest
    - (D) too fast

18. Tom spoke so _____ that I couldn't hear his words.
    - (A) noisy
    - (B) quiet
    - (C) hard
    - (D) quietly

19. This medicine doesn't taste _____.
    - (A) bitter
    - (B) bitterly
    - (C) well
    - (D) much

20. _____, the storm damage was not serious.

    (A) Luck   (B) Luckiest

    (C) Luckier   (D) Luckily

21. We have some clubs at our school, but not _____.

    (A) very   (B) so many

    (C) a few   (D) much

22. The sales manager had to cancel the appointment with his client at the last minute as an urgent _____ came up at his office.

    (A) action   (B) incident

    (C) matter   (D) trouble

23. This year the company plans to _____ on fewer college graduates.

    (A) get   (B) work

    (C) employ   (D) take

24. Some people would like to _____ all the rules, but that would be dangerous.

    (A) do away with   (B) away

    (C) do with   (D) do away

Part 6 ⟋ Text Completion

Read the text that follows. A word, phrase, or sentence is missing in parts of the text. Select the best answer to complete the text.

● Questions 25-28 refer to the following information.

Ideas for Painting your Bookshelf

You may paint your bookshelf _____ you put it together. However,
    25.

be careful not _____ inside the holes for the screws. If this happens,
        26.

please remove the _____ paint before putting the bookshelf together.
        27.

If you don't plan on painting your bookshelf at all, we recommend at least

brushing it with an oil-based primer. _____.
            28.

25. (A) after
    (B) before
    (C) during
    (D) next

26. (A) painted
    (B) painting
    (C) paints
    (D) to paint

27. (A) extra
    (B) few
    (C) less
    (D) more

28. (A) If you read many books, you will need a bookshelf.
    (B) There are seven shelves in our largest bookshelf.
    (C) This will make your bookshelf easier to clean.
    (D) You can find bookshelves of all sizes at our store.

Read the following selection of texts. Select the best answer for each question.

●Questions 29-33 refer to the following agenda and e-mail.

City Transportation Board Meeting
March 24
7:30 p.m.

Reading of last month's meeting minutes for approval

Reports from directors	Ben Anderson	New bus routes
	Sheryl McFadden	Public relations
	Richard Percival	Metro extension

Voting   Review candidates for new commissioner and choose one

Open Forum

    - Wildlife Rescue has concerns about the location of the new subway lines.

    - The Mayor will present his proposal to renovate the bus terminal downtown.

    - An environmental group has questions about buying new city buses.

To: Walter J. Riley <walterriley@lawtoncity.gov.org>
From: Alice Dolby <liced@berryville.net>
Date: March 26
Subject: City buses

Dear Transportation Commissioner,

Congratulations on your new appointment. Our organization, Green Fields, has been fighting air pollution in Lawton City for many years. The city introduced the first electric bus five years ago and we were told then that all city buses would be replaced by electric buses. Of course, we were disappointed to hear at the March 24th board meeting that there is no money to buy any more electric buses. But we have an idea to get money for these buses. Just raise the public parking fees by 25 percent, and you could buy two new buses each year. Green Fields would be happy to work with your public relations person on a campaign to support this good idea.

Thank you,

Alice Dolby

29. Who is worried about the metro extension?

    (A) Alice Dolby

    (B) Green Fields

    (C) Richard Percival

    (D) Wildlife Rescue

30. When did the city introduce the new electric buses?

    (A) This year

    (B) Last year

    (C) Three years ago

    (D) Five years ago

31. How does Ms. Dolby suggest the city raise money to buy more buses?

    (A) By collecting volunteer donations

    (B) By increasing public parking rates

    (C) By postponing the construction of new stations

    (D) By requesting businesses sponsor the buses

32. When was the issue Ms. Dolby was interested in discussed at the board meeting?

    (A) At the end of the Open Forum

    (B) Before 7:30

    (C) Prior to the directors' reports

    (D) Shortly after the election

33. Who might Green Fields work with on the campaign, according to the e-mail?

    (A) Ben Anderson

    (B) Sheryl McFadden

    (C) The mayor

    (D) Walter Riley

文法チェック ✔

●形容詞・副詞と比較

A. 形容詞と副詞には、比較のための変化形（比較級「より〜」と最上級「もっとも〜」）があります。形容詞の最上級にはふつうtheがつきます。

B. 形容詞と副詞の比較変化のうちでも、特に不規則に変化する場合に注意しましょう。

例：good [well] – better – best、bad [ill] – worse – worst、many [much] – more – most、little – less – least、late – later / latter – latest / last、far – farther / further – farthest / furthest、など

C. 比較級や最上級を強めるには、muchやevenなどを用います（veryは用いません）。

D. 副詞の主な役割は動詞や形容詞や他の副詞を修飾することですが、文全体を修飾することもあります。同じ副詞でも、文中での位置によって、何を修飾するのかが変わってくることがあります。

例：They got married and lived *happily*. ［動詞を修飾］

（彼らは、結婚し、幸せに暮らした）

例：*Happily*, no one was injured. ［文全体を修飾］

（幸いにも、けがをした人はいなかった）

学習のヒント

　リーディング・セクションでは、75分の解答時間を各パートにどのように配分するかも重要です。パート5と6では1問30秒以内で、パート7では1問1分以内で、それぞれ解答するのが標準的な時間配分です。パート5が30秒×30問＝15分、パート6が30秒×16問＝8分、パート7が1分×54問＝54分だと計77分になってしまいますから、実際にはパート5や6のできるだけ多くの問題でもっと短い時間で解答することができるようにしておかなければなりません。1つの問題に時間をかけすぎると、結局どんどん時間がなくなります。最後の問題まで行き着けず、解いていたら正解できたはずの問題を解き逃したりします。焦って余計な誤りを犯してしまうこともあります。時間がなくなると悪いことばかりです。

　75分の試験時間内にすべての問題に解答することが重要です。問題ごとの制限時間を超えてしまったら、適当にマークして次の問題に進む、といった「英断」もときには重要になります。問題を解くことに集中すると時間の経過もついつい忘れがちですが、この点も意識して練習してみてください。たとえば、このテキストの予習をするときにも、ぜひ、まずは時間を決めて解いてみてください。

Unit 10

🎧 LISTENING

●●● Warm-up & Vocabulary Build-up ●●●

英文を聴きとって、空所にあてはまる単語を下の選択肢から選んで入れなさい。

1. The _____ basket is full of clothes.
2. The bag of _____ includes fruits and vegetables.
3. How much should I _____ this picture of the poster?
4. Where can I _____ my dollars for euros?
5. Did the repairman _____ the copier this afternoon?
6. Keep your _____ with you at all times.
7. Please _____ returned library books here.
8. There are _____ on each floor of our hotel.

   a. belongings   **b.** deposit   **c.** enlarge   **d.** exchange

   e. fix   **f.** groceries   **g.** laundry   **h.** restrooms

---

Part 1 **Photographs**

You will hear four short statements. Look at the picture, and select the statement that best describes what you see in the picture.

1.

(A) (B) (C) (D)

2.

(A) (B) (C) (D)

Part 2 **Question-Response**

You will hear a question or statement and three responses. Listen carefully, and select the best response to the question or statement.

3. (A) (B) (C)
4. (A) (B) (C)
5. (A) (B) (C)
6 (A) (B) (C)
7. (A) (B) (C)

You will hear a short conversation between two people. Listen carefully, and select the best response to each question.

8. What does the man ask the woman to do?
   - (A) Change rooms
   - (B) Delay her flight
   - (C) Fill out a questionnaire
   - (D) Share her table

9. Where will the woman go in 15 minutes?
   - (A) The airport
   - (B) The hotel
   - (C) A meeting room
   - (D) A restaurant

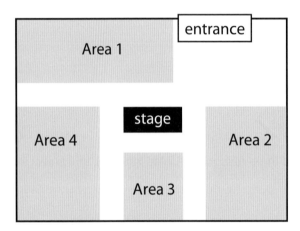

10. What does the man ask the woman for?
    - (A) Help with a form
    - (B) Her advice
    - (C) Her signature
    - (D) A ride to the show

11. Look at the graphic. Where does the woman think the booth should be this year?
    - (A) Area 1
    - (B) Area 2
    - (C) Area 3
    - (D) Area 4

Part 4   Talks

You will hear a short talk given by a single speaker. Listen carefully, and select the best response to each question.

12. What did the deer eat?

    (A) The farm animals

    (B) The farmer's crops

    (C) Nothing

    (D) The farm animals' food

Room Schedule	
Clover	Capital Equities
Dandelion	Knight Read Estate
Rose	Monroe & Partners
Tulip	Jasper Company

13. What is the speaker talking about?

    (A) A change in attendee numbers

    (B) A change in meeting days

    (C) A change in price

    (D) A change in weather

14. Look at the graphic. Which room will Monroe & Partners use?

    (A) Clover

    (B) Dandelion

    (C) Rose

    (D) Tulip

READING

空所にあてはまる単語を、下の選択肢から選んで入れなさい。

1.   These packages should be sent by air _____.
2.   None of the people applying for the job is _____.
3.   The hotel will _____ you to a free breakfast.
4.   Sixteen teams will _____ in the tournament.
5.   Use this form to _____ which items you are ordering.
6.   Here is a _____ on how to make soups tastier.
7.   After you _____ these figures, record them all on the computer.
8.   Does that article talk about business _____?

a. compete	**b.** compile	**c.** freight	**d.** indicate
e. issues	**f.** qualified	**g.** tip	**h.** treat

Part 5   Incomplete Sentences

A word or phrase is missing in each of the sentences. Select the best answer to complete each sentence.

15. If this model is too expensive, we have _____ brand.

(A) another   (B) other

(C) some   (D) any

16. _____ does the library allow you to keep a book when you check it out?

(A) What time   (B) How many

(C) What length   (D) How long

17. _____ do you think we should go to the concert tonight?

(A) What   (B) How

(C) Which   (D) Who

18. The test ran _____, so the results are very good.

(A) perfected   (B) perfection

(C) perfect   (D) perfectly

19. It was entirely _____ the holiday that the airport was crowded.

(A) so that   (B) such that

(C) even if   (D) because of

20. In the section chief's opinion, nothing stood out _____ all the ideas that were presented at the brainstorming session.

(A) among
(B) nevertheless
(C) owing to
(D) so far

21. Our oldest son is old _____ to look after himself.

(A) already
(B) as
(C) enough
(D) much

22. The store has never recorded _____ low sales for a new CD.

(A) every
(B) such
(C) that
(D) those

23. If you don't have a driver's license _____ ID card, then present your credit card and tax receipt at registration.

(A) either
(B) neither
(C) nor
(D) or

24. Fifty people _____ can be seated in the back dining room.

(A) more than
(B) mostly
(C) at most
(D) no more

Read the text that follows. A word, phrase, or sentence is missing in parts of the text. Select the best answer to complete the text.

●Questions 25-28 refer to the following memo.

To: All Employees
From: Susanna Grisham, President
Re: New Vice President of Sales
Date: March 3

We are pleased to announce the _____ of Fred Brandt to Vice President of
                                                            25.
Sales. In the past twelve months, Mr. Brandt has provided great service to our clients,

_____ in several new accounts and demonstrated excellent sales leadership.
        26.

_____. He will start his new position on April 4 in Suite 25 on the sixth floor.
    27.
Please join me in congratulating Mr. Brandt _____ his new position.
                                                                    28.

25. (A) promote
        (B) promoting
        (C) promotion
        (D) promotional

26. (A) brought
        (B) is bringing
        (C) was brought
        (D) will bring

27. (A) Mr. Brandt will be doing a lot of golf and gardening after he leaves.
        (B) Our company has grown substantially because of Mr. Brandt's work.
        (C) Please pack your things in the boxes provided to prepare for the move.
        (D) This quarter sales have gone down to concerning levels, unfortunately.

28. (A) in
        (B) on
        (C) to
        (D) with

Part 7 — Reading Comprehension

Read the following selection of texts. Select the best answer for each question.

● Questions 29-33 refer to the following invoice and e-mail.

Office Warehouse, Inc.

Sold To:	Ship To:	Date:
Hawkins, Murphy, et al 4567 W. 15th Avenue Chicago, IL 65007	Elaine Percival Hawkins, Murphy, et al 4567 W. 15th Avenue Chicago, IL 65007	June 30

INVOICE	Number 347	COPY

Description	Quantity	Unit Price	Total Price
XPress-copy machine	1	$1,200.00	$1,200.00
L-shaped desk	1	$750.00	$750.00

Payment due no later than 30 days from date of delivery

NOTES: Customer requires setup of both items.

Total before discount	$1,950.00
10% discount	$195.00
5% tax	$87.75
Shipping fee	$50.00
GRAND TOTAL	$1,892.75

To: Chuck Whitmore <cwhitmore@officewarehouse.net>
From: Elaine Percival <epercival@hawkins.net>
Date: July 2
Subject: Invoice 347

Dear Mr. Whitmore,

We received our order yesterday and have been pleased with the copier's performance so far. Your delivery people were helpful in setting it up and explaining how to use it. I do have a concern about the invoice. As you remember, we have a frequent-user discount on all of our orders. But, due to the problems with our previous order (Invoice 346), you promised an additional discount off our next order. Therefore, we should have received a 15-percent discount for the items on this current invoice. Please send the corrected invoice to me as soon as possible. Also, your delivery staff forgot to leave your new catalog when they came. Could you send one along with the invoice?
Thank you for your attention to this matter.

Sincerely,

Elaine Percival
Office Manager

29. When should Ms. Percival pay for the items, according to the invoice?
    (A) At the time of delivery
    (B) By the end of July
    (C) No later than June 30th
    (D) Two weeks after delivery

30. How does Ms. Percival feel about the XPress?
    (A) Angry
    (B) Disappointed
    (C) Satisfied
    (D) Surprised

31. The word "concern" in paragraph 2, line 1 of the e-mail, is closest in meaning to…?
    (A) Business
    (B) Interest
    (C) Relationship
    (D) Worry

32. What did Mr. Whitmore offer to Ms. Percival after their previous order?
    (A) 10-percent off
    (B) An extra 5-percent discount
    (C) Free delivery
    (D) Free product assembly

33. What does Ms. Percival request in her e-mail?
    (A) A payment extension
    (B) Copy machine maintenance
    (C) Replacement of one of her items
    (D) Updated product information

文法チェック ✔

●不定代名詞—another と other

A. another と other は、one や some と対比的に用いられ、one や some で取り除いた残りを指し示します。代名詞としても、名詞の修飾語としても、用いることができます。

B. another は、「残りのうちの一人、一つ」を指し示します。

例：I don't like this one; show me *another*.

（これは気に入らないので、別のを見せてください）

C. 「残りの最後の一人、一つ」を指し示すには the other を用います。

例：I bought three books. I have already read two of them and will read *the other* tomorrow.

（本を3冊買ったが、2冊は読んでしまったので、明日最後の1冊を読むつもりだ）

D. 「残りのうちの複数人、複数個」を指し示すには others を用います。名詞を修飾する場合は「other＋複数名詞」の形になります。

例： Some students like the teacher; *others* (＝ other students) hate him.

（その先生を好きな生徒もいれば、嫌っている生徒もいる）

E. 「残りの全員、全部」を指し示すには the others を用います。名詞を修飾する場合は「the other＋複数名詞」の形になります。

例：Here are many books. Some are novels, but *the others* (＝ the other books) are comics.

（ここにたくさん本があり、一部は小説だが、残りは全部漫画だ）

学習のヒント

　パート7については、ユニット9の「学習のヒント」で「標準時間は1問1分」と言いましたが、実は、特に入門レベルの学習者にとってはそれ以上の時間を必要とする設問も多くあります。逆に、入門レベルの学習者であっても、時間さえかければ正解できる場合も少なくありません。そのための時間を確保するためには、パート5と6をできるだけ迅速に解答してゆくことが大切になります。もちろん正確さも重要です。パート5と6をできるだけ正確かつ迅速に解答していけるよう、語いや熟語、語法、文法事項についての知識をできるだけたくさん身につけましょう。パート5や6では、文全体の意味や文脈をあまり考えなくても、単純な知識だけで、極端な場合はほんの数秒で解ける問題もけっして少なくありません。

Unit 11

🎧 LISTENING

●●● Warm-up & Vocabulary Build-up ●●●

英文を聴きとって、空所にあてはまる単語を下の選択肢から選んで入れなさい。

1. The apartment building is ten _____ tall.
2. How many people did you _____ to the party?
3. Can we _____ the old sign with a new one?
4. That box is _____ heavy, so take care.
5. The manual _____ the correct tire pressure.
6. One _____ of this cell phone is a large touch screen.
7. We offer quality service at _____ prices.
8. We have a large _____ of exciting new toys!

a. describes	**b.** feature	**c.** invite	**d.** moderate
e. pretty	**f.** quantity	**g.** replace	**h.** stories

Part 1 **Photographs**

You will hear four short statements. Look at the picture, and select the statement that best describes what you see in the picture.

1.

(A) (B) (C) (D)

2.

(A)　(B)　(C)　(D)

Part 2　Question-Response

You will hear a question or statement and three responses. Listen carefully, and select the best response to the question or statement.

3.　(A)　(B)　(C)

4.　(A)　(B)　(C)

5.　(A)　(B)　(C)

6.　(A)　(B)　(C)

7.　(A)　(B)　(C)

You will hear a short conversation between two people. Listen carefully, and select the best response to each question.

8. What does the woman want to buy?
    (A) A bed
    (B) A couch
    (C) A set of dishes
    (D) A table and chairs

9. Why will the woman need to pay $50?
    (A) For a different color
    (B) For quick delivery
    (C) For taxes
    (D) For the nicer fabric

Type	People	Bags
compact	up to 4	1-2
sedan	up to 5	2-4
SUV	up to 7	3-5
truck	up to 2	4

10. Where most likely are the speakers?
    (A) At an airport
    (B) At a bus depot
    (C) At a ferry terminal
    (D) At a train station

11. Look at the graphic. Which type of car will the man rent?
    (A) A compact
    (B) A sedan
    (C) An SUV
    (D) A truck

Part 4 Talks

You will hear a short talk given by a single speaker. Listen carefully, and select the best response to each question.

12. What does Mike ask Ms. Owens to do?
- (A) Meet him at the airport
- (B) Send a messenger to his office
- (C) Reschedule the meeting
- (D) Take the next flight

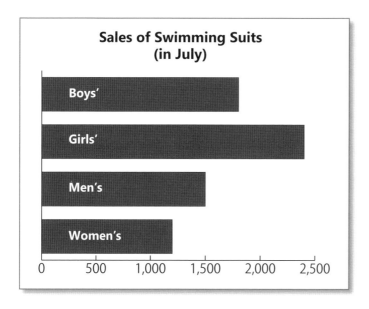

13. Why did some suits sell well in July?
- (A) Customers liked the suit colors.
- (B) A free gift was offered.
- (C) Prices were discounted.
- (D) The weather was especially hot.

14. Look at the graphic. Which item will listeners discuss now?
- (A) Boys' swimming suits
- (B) Girls' swimming suits
- (C) Men's swimming suits
- (D) Women's swimming suits

📖 READING

● ● ● Vocabulary Build-up ● ● ●

空所にあてはまる単語を、下の選択肢から選んで入れなさい。

1. He was _____ after the long hike.
2. Each _____ serving has only one gram of fat.
3. Our canned coffee _____ the best selling one on the market.
4. This coupon is _____ until March 31.
5. Book your room early to _____ you get your first choice.
6. To _____ your safety, please wear your seatbelt.
7. This computer manual can serve as a _____ if questions arise.
8. Light comes through the _____ window.

a. ensure	**b.** exhausted	**c.** individual	**d.** insure
e. reference	**f.** remains	**g.** transparent	**h.** valid

Part 5 — Incomplete Sentences

A word or phrase is missing in each of the sentences. Select the best answer to complete each sentence.

15. A genius is a person _____ is very intelligent.
    (A) who   (B) whose
    (C) whom   (D) which

16. _____ taking this medicine, do not drive.
    (A) Since   (B) After
    (C) Because   (D) Already

17. _____ Alice did not study, she received a good score on the test.
    (A) Because   (B) If
    (C) When   (D) Though

18. Seats at the back of the hall _____ have anyone in them.
    (A) hard   (B) very
    (C) seldom   (D) much

19. The newest car was too _____, so most people could not buy it.
    (A) wealthy   (B) expensive
    (C) priced   (D) free

20. My mother is _____ capable of taking over my father's business while he is away.

    (A) enough   (B) too

    (C) bit   (D) quite

21. The brass band concert begins _____ one hour.

    (A) to   (B) for

    (C) by   (D) in

22. The landlord agreed to _____ a certain part of the lease contract after the tenant strongly objected to it.

    (A) adjust   (B) amend

    (C) reform   (D) retrieve

23. Some shoppers stick _____ the same brands loyally for years.

    (A) at   (B) on

    (C) in   (D) to

24. Several guests settled _____ pizza and salad for dinner that night.

    (A) at   (B) on

    (C) to   (D) of

Read the text that follows. A word, phrase, or sentence is missing in parts of the text. Select the best answer to complete the text.

●Questions 25-28 refer to the following notice.

You _____ for a credit card from Yellow Bank International. You
　　　　　25.

_____ need to fill out the enclosed application and wait four weeks for your
　　26.

card to be sent. _____. You will enjoy a $10,000 credit limit and a low interest
　　　　　　27.

rate. We will also give you a $100 cash rebate on your first _____ using your
　　　　　　　　　　　　　　　　　　　　　　　28.

new card.

25. (A) have approved
　　　(B) have been approved
　　　(C) have been approving
　　　(D) will be approving

26. (A) formally
　　　(B) lastly
　　　(C) mostly
　　　(D) simply

27. (A) If you win the contest, you will get a $500 gift card.
　　　(B) There are no monthly fees or activation charges.
　　　(C) These cards can be used for entry into all museums.
　　　(D) You can buy our sweater set for just $59, plus tax.

28. (A) discount
　　　(B) purchase
　　　(C) rental
　　　(D) visit

Part 7　Reading Comprehension

Read the following selection of texts. Select the best answer for each question.

● Questions 29-33 refer to the following review and letter.

Reviewed in this issue:
Spartan Computer Backpack from Vargus

For those who commute to work on foot or by bicycle like I do, I found a good computer backpack by Vargus. There are two sizes: the Toledo is for screens up to 17" and the Spartan is made for 15" laptops like mine. What I like about the Spartan is the color scheme: no loud colors, just practical black and gray combination, with a reflective stripe for night-time safety. And it comes with storage for everything you need daily. It includes a cellphone pocket, a water bottle pocket and a place for your keys and coins. Compared to other similar products, Vargus's prices are quite reasonable. The packs are $39.99 for the medium and $59.99 for the large.

Dear Editor,

Regarding the computer backpacks reviewed in the June issue of *Computing Monthly*, I'd like to point some things out to your readers. I travel a lot in my work as a journalist and have tried several different packs for my computer, though none from Vargus. I have been disappointed by all of them since they are very heavy, even before the computer goes in. As for the color scheme, who wants a bag with the same dull colors as everyone else's? Not me!

Isabel Quince

29. What is NOT a feature of the Spartan?

    (A) It can hold a 17-inch laptop.

    (B) It has a cellphone pocket.

    (C) It has a place to store keys.

    (D) It has a reflective stripe.

30. According to the review, what is good about the Spartan, compared to other backpacks?

    (A) Its material

    (B) Its price

    (C) Its size

    (D) Its weight

31. Who is Ms. Quince?

    (A) A backpack designer

    (B) A reporter

    (C) A reviewer of *Computing Monthly*

    (D) A Vargus employee

32. What do the reviewer and Ms. Quince have in common?

    (A) They bike to work.

    (B) They carry their laptops to work.

    (C) They have already bought a Toledo.

    (D) They like Vargus backpacks.

33. Why would Ms. Quince NOT likely purchase a Spartan?

    (A) It is not waterproof.

    (B) It is too big for her.

    (C) She would not like the color.

    (D) She needs a pack with wheels.

文法チェック ✓

●関係詞（1）

A. 「私が昨日見た人」のように、文「私が昨日見た」が名詞「人」を修飾する場合、関係詞を用います。関係詞には関係代名詞と関係副詞があります。

B. 関係代名詞は、代名詞の仲間ですから、文の中で主語、補語、（動詞や前置詞の）目的語、（whoseの形で）名詞の修飾語になります。また、普通の代名詞（I、my、me）のように、文中の働きに応じて形が変わります。動詞や前置詞の目的語になる場合には、省略されることがあります。

例：That is the man (*that / whom*) I saw yesterday. ［動詞の目的語］
　　（あれが、私が昨日見た人です）

また、修飾される名詞（「先行詞」と言います）に応じて（「人」か「人以外」か）、使い分けが必要になる場合があります。

C. 関係副詞は、副詞の仲間ですから、文の中で動詞の修飾要素になります。先行詞が「場所」ならwhere、「時」ならwhen、「理由」ならwhy、「方法」ならhowを、それぞれ用います。

例：Saturday is the <u>day</u> *when* we go shopping. ［先行詞が時］
　　（土曜日は、私たちが買い物に行く日です）

D. パート5のような問題では、関係代名詞と関係副詞のどちらを用いるかがポイントになります。次の例では、空所の後にisの主語がないので、関係代名詞のwhichかthatを補うのが正解です。先行詞が「場所」を表すplaceだからといって単純に関係副詞のwhereを補ってしまうような誤りには注意してください。

例：Our town is the place (　) is well known for its beautiful nature.
　　（私たちの町は、美しい自然でよく知られているところです）

学習のヒント

　ここまでの練習で見てきたように、パート6と7では、電子メール、短いメッセージのやり取り、オンライン・チャット、ウェブ・ページ、手紙、FAX文書、掲示、広告、新聞や雑誌の記事、報告書、レストランのメニューなどさまざまな種類の英語の文書が素材にされています。これらの文書では、文書の種類によって独特のスタイルや文体が用いられている場合があります。こういったスタイルや文体に慣れておけば、問題がより解きやすくなります。ユニット1からもう一度見直しておくとよいでしょう。さらに、こういった知識には、実生活に活かせるものもたくさんあります。パート2と3についても同じようなことを言いましたが、TOEIC®対策をTOEIC®対策だけに終わらせず、パート6と7については、ぜひ一種の「文例集」としても活用してみてください。

Unit 12

●●● Warm-up & Vocabulary Build-up ●●●

英文を聴きとって、空所にあてはまる単語を下の選択肢から選んで入れなさい。

1. A bicycle is chained to the bridge's _____.
2. There are huge _____ supporting the building.
3. Did you _____ why the printer wasn't working?
4. Put the tent and the other camping _____ into the car.
5. Did you _____ some money from the ATM?
6. The water park's newest _____ is a large water slide.
7. This pocket knife can be _____ in many ways.
8. Creating this type of jewelry is a fine _____.

a. attraction	**b.** columns	**c.** craft	**d.** discover
e. gear	**f.** railing	**g.** useful	**h.** withdraw

Part 1　Photographs

You will hear four short statements. Look at the picture, and select the statement that best describes what you see in the picture.

1.

(A)　(B)　(C)　(D)

2.

(A) (B) (C) (D)

Part 2 **Question-Response**

You will hear a question or statement and three responses. Listen carefully, and select the best response to the question or statement.

3. (A) (B) (C)

4. (A) (B) (C)

5. (A) (B) (C)

6. (A) (B) (C)

7. (A) (B) (C)

You will hear a short conversation between two people. Listen carefully, and select the best response to each question.

8. What does the man say about changing jobs?
- (A) He likes the new town.
- (B) He wants a promotion.
- (C) He wants to be closer to his family.
- (D) He wants to see different cities.

9. What kind of skills does the woman say the job requires?
- (A) Communication
- (B) Presentation
- (C) Research
- (D) Technology

4th floor	Jenkins, Inc.
3rd floor	Jenkins, Inc.
2nd floor	Klein & Associates
1st floor	reception

10. What is the woman delivering to the building?
- (A) Some documents
- (B) Some flowers
- (C) Some food
- (D) Some supplies

11. Look at the graphic. Which floor will the woman go to?
- (A) The first
- (B) The second
- (C) The third
- (D) The fourth

Part 4 **Talks**

You will hear a short talk given by a single speaker. Listen carefully, and select the best response to each question.

12. Where would people hear this request?

    (A) At a movie theater box office

    (B) In an airport departure lounge

    (C) At a restaurant coat check

    (D) At a concert hall

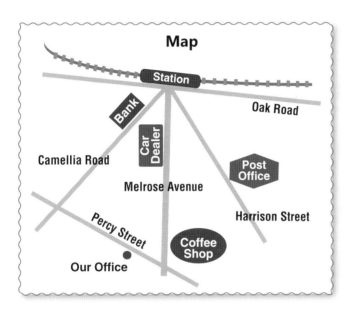

13. Why is the speaker meeting Mr. Johnson tomorrow?

    (A) To congratulate him

    (B) To discuss a product

    (C) To interview him

    (D) To talk about a project

14. Look at the graphic. What will Mr. Johnson pass on the way to Oleson Design?

    (A) A bank

    (B) A car dealer

    (C) A coffee shop

    (D) A post office

●●● Vocabulary Build-up ●●●

空所にあてはまる単語を、下の選択肢から選んで入れなさい。

1. _____ a large onion and then add it to the water.
2. The _____ of this dish are listed below.
3. The _____ of Flight 096 is Dallas.
4. Lift tickets are $38.00 for the _____ day.
5. Average _____ for this area are listed below.
6. The total _____ of the order is $120.50.
7. You need to pay $1.50 per each _____ hour.
8. Come see our new _____ of gardening products.

a. additional	**b.** amount	**c.** destination	**d.** dice
e. entire	**f.** ingredients	**g.** line	**h.** temperatures

Part 5   Incomplete Sentences

A word or phrase is missing in each of the sentences. Select the best answer to complete each sentence.

15. The following is one of the questions that _____ on the test yesterday.
- (A) has been
- (B) have been
- (C) was
- (D) were

16. How long _____ the next train departs?
- (A) will
- (B) when
- (C) until
- (D) does

17. The map was detailed, _____ it contained no references to his hometown.
- (A) if
- (B) because
- (C) as
- (D) yet

18. I have to run an errand tomorrow morning, so I may be a _____ late.
- (A) small
- (B) few
- (C) little
- (D) briefly

19. Rachel is such a _____ person that she often gets her feelings hurt.
- (A) sensible
- (B) sensitive
- (C) sense
- (D) senseless

20. We ask for your patience _____ this period of renovation.

    (A) during   (B) since

    (C) while   (D) as

21. Utility rates are falling _____ reduced energy prices.

    (A) because of   (B) although

    (C) so   (D) in spite of

22. The committee worked _____ the ideas one by one.

    (A) at   (B) with

    (C) through   (D) over

23. A cut in prices allowed the company to _____ onto market share.

    (A) hold   (B) retain

    (C) restore   (D) keep

24. _____ the convention center opened, it burned down.

    (A) For the day   (B) All day long

    (C) The very day   (D) Throughout the day

Read the text that follows. A word, phrase, or sentence is missing in parts of the text. Select the best answer to complete the text.

●Questions 25-28 refer to the following information.

PRINCE LEATHER

Thank you for choosing a Prince Leather journal. We are located on Mt. Angel Island,

_____ craftsmanship is a way of life. Our leather journals, photo albums,
    25.

organizers, and accessories are all _____. _____. But if you do not, please
                    26.   **27.**

return it to our workshop and we will repair or replace it _____ question.
                                     28.

25. (A) when
    (B) where
    (C) which
    (D) whose

26. (A) handmade
    (B) handout
    (C) handshake
    (D) handsome

27. (A) After the interview, we felt your experience in leatherwork and design is a good fit for our workshop.
    (B) Please return the damaged product to us and let us know if you would like a new one or a refund.
    (C) These books can be used as memo pads or calendars, and paper refills can be added when needed.
    (D) We are confident you will appreciate the thoughtful design and handcrafted quality of this journal.

28. (A) by
    (B) into
    (C) with
    (D) without

Read the following selection of texts. Select the best answer for each question.

●Questions 29-33 refer to the following advertisement, online shopping cart, and e-mail.

NEW and IMPROVED EASY-TO-USE WEBSITE

Bevin's Home Improvement has made some improvements to its online shopping experience. Our website has been redesigned, making all of our products easier to find and add to your cart. We've also added a Live Chat feature, which means you can ask questions about our products in real time. It's almost like being in the store talking to one of our knowledgeable sales clerks. To celebrate our new look, we've made shipping free for orders over $200. There's never been a better time to make those changes in your home you've been putting off. Visit *www.bevinshome.com* today!

Bevin's Home Improvement
bevinshome.com/ shopping cart

Order Summary No. 593
Customer: Ed Kohl

Item	Qty.	Price Ea.	Total
BHI-385 Paint rollers	3	$10.50	$31.50
BHI-396 Paint brushes	5	$8.99	$44.95
BHI-047 Light lavender paint — gallon	2	$45.00	$90.00
BHI-189 French flowers border — roll	3	$15.00	$45.00
		Subtotal	$211.45
		Tax	$21.14
		Shipping	FREE
		Total	**$232.59**

To: Customer Service <cs@bevinshome.com>

From: Ed Kohl <ekohl@mostmail.com>

Date: September 9

Subject: Order 593

Hi there,

I just received my order today and I was surprised that it only took two days. Thanks for the fast delivery. One problem though: the quantities of BHI-189 and BHI-047 appear to have been switched. This means I can't start on my home project this three-day weekend like I planned. Bummer. Please send the missing item as soon as possible.

Thanks in advance for taking care of this for me.

Ed Kohl

29. What are customers encouraged to do on the website?
- (A) Check the discount section
- (B) Compare prices with competitors'
- (C) Find paint colors they like
- (D) Use a virtual assistant

30. What is true of Bevin's Home Improvement?
- (A) It has a physical store.
- (B) It is sold out of paint supplies.
- (C) It offers overnight shipping.
- (D) It recently opened an online store.

31. Why did Mr. Kohl receive free shipping?
- (A) He had a problem with a previous order.
- (B) He is a repeat customer.
- (C) He spent over a certain amount.
- (D) He used a special coupon.

32. What did Mr. Kohl receive in error?
- (A) Three gallons of paint
- (B) Three paint brushes
- (C) Three rolls of border
- (D) Five paint rollers

33. What was Mr. Kohl planning to do this weekend?
- (A) Go on a trip
- (B) Hold a house party
- (C) Improve his house
- (D) Relax outside

文法チェック ✔

●関係詞（2）

A. 関係代名詞のthatは、先行詞が「人」でも「人以外」でも用いることができる便利な関係代名詞ですが、所有格がありません。また、非制限用法（先行詞と関係詞の間にカンマがある用法）で用いることができません。

　　例：I visited Tom, who (×that) was not at home.
　　　　（トムを訪ねたが、家にはいなかった）

B. 関係代名詞が主語の場合、その後の動詞の形は先行詞の人称や数に合わせます。

C. 特殊な関係代名詞にwhatがあります。普通の関係代名詞は、名詞（先行詞）を修飾する、形容詞の働きをする語群をつくりますが、関係代名詞のwhatで始まる語群は名詞の働きをします。次の例では、what you are saying全体が動詞understandの目的語になっています。なお、what you are sayingの中でwhatはsayの目的語になっていますが、この点は普通の関係代名詞と同じです。

　　例：I can't understand *what* you are saying.
　　　　（私には君の言っていることがわからない）

学習のヒント

　このテキストで学習することだけでも、単語や文法事項をはじめとして、相当な勉強量になると思います。まずは、しっかり復習をして、テキストで学習したことを完璧に身につけてください。単語や文法事項など、知識として身につけなければならない部分は、しっかりと定着させてください。ただ、正直なところ、練習量としてはこのテキストだけでは十分とは言えません。よく言われることだと思いますが、知っているからと言って必ずしも問題が解けるわけではありません。知識を実際に活用できるようにするには、それ相応の練習が必要です。TOEIC® Listening & Reading Testについても、できるだけたくさん問題を解いてみることが、遠回りのようで結局はいちばんの近道です。

　ぜひ、TOEIC® Listening & Reading Testの問題集を別に1冊用意してみてください。少々大きめの書店に行けば、TOEIC® Listening & Reading Testの問題集がところ狭しと並んでいると思います。また、CD付きでも比較的安価に入手できるはずです。価格やレベルも含めて気に入ったものでけっこうです。授業の担当教員が勧めてくれたものなどがある場合は、それでもよいと思います。できれば、授業と並行させて、主に復習用として使ってみてください。知識として必要な部分については、定着や強化を促進できるはずです。また、特にリスニング・セクションについては、問題への取り組み方の練習になるはずです。

新訂版　TOEIC® L&R テストへようこそ

検印省略	2020年1月31日　初版 2023年1月31日　第3刷発行
編著者	北原　良夫
発行者	原　　雅久
発行所	株式会社 朝日出版社
	〒101-0065 東京都千代田区西神田3-3-5
	電話　東京　(03) 3239-0271
	FAX　東京　(03) 3239-0479
	e-mail text-e@asahipress.com
	振替口座　00140-2-46008
	http://www.asahipress.com/
	製版／錦明印刷

乱丁・落丁本はお取り替えいたします。
ISBN 978-4-255-15649-1 C1082